Ceramic Arts Studio
Mike Schneider

Thousands of collectors will rejoice in this new guide to Ceramic Arts Studio. Started in Madison, Wisconsin in the late 1930s or early 1940s, the company, from 1942 to 1955, focused on the production of slipcast figurines instead of its initial hand-thrown decorative wares. These figurines are avidly collected today.

The figurine enterprise began when a secretary employed by the state of Wisconsin, Betty Harrington, made a figurine of a kneeling nude woman with some clay her young daughters had given her. Early in 1942 she took the figurine to the fledgling Ceramic Arts Studio to see about the possibility of getting it glazed and fired. Rueben Sand not only accommodated her, he asked her to model additional figurines for him. That began a relationship which lasted throughout the life of the business, a relationship from which today's collectors are still reaping the benefits.

In over 250 color photographs Mike Schneider captures the beauty and charm of these works, providing a reference that has long been needed by collectors. The photographs are accompanied by a wealth of useful hints on care, repair, preservation, valuing, fakes and reproductions. The figurines are organized by type with sections on People, The Animal Kingdom, Fantasies, Posy Pots, Decorating the Walls, and Miscellaneous. The Price Guide will be an important tool for the collector, whether novice or experienced.

About the Author

Mike Schneider is a freelance writer whose previous works for Schiffer include *The Complete Salt and Pepper Shaker Book* and *The Complete Cookie Jar Book*, both of which have won high praise from collectors and reviewers.

CERAMIC ARTS STUDIO

Identification and Price Guide

Mike Schneider

Schiffer Publishing Ltd

77 Lower Valley Road, Atglen, PA 19310

Dedication

This book is dedicated to Betty Harrington, Louise Bauer, Kay Finch, Laura Taylor Hughes, Hedi Schoop, Ruth Van Tellingen Bendel, Florence Ward and the scores of other women both living and dead--and largely unsung--whose talent for designing and modeling during the Depression, World War II and the postwar years have given today's collectors of mid-twentieth century American pottery so much enjoyment.

Above Photo: According to the 1954 catalog, these *Fish* salt and peppers were made in one treatment only: "yellow, green and rose colors blended." On all of them that I have seen the blending apparently caused the rose to come out brown. The one on the left stands 3 3/4 inches high, while its mate on the right goes 4 inches. Both have Ceramic Arts Studio marks. *King Collection.*

Title Page Photo: Close examination of the photograph on the preceding page, *Alice* and the *March Hare*, will reveal many of the factors that led to Ceramic Arts Studio's success: reasonably priced, well modeled and competently decorated people and animal figurines of popular subjects that caught the public's fancy. During chaotic times people across America could lay down anywhere from a few cents to a few dollars, and gain repeated, if temporary, aesthetic distraction from more serious matters such as Bataan, the Lutwaffe, frozen Chosin and the hydrogen bomb. *Alice* is 4 7/8 inches high, has a Betty Harrington/Ceramic Arts Studio mark along with the name *Alice.* The *March Hare*, 6 inches high, is marked similarly, its mark including the words *March Hare. Oravitz Collection.*

Attitude and *Arabesque*, referred to in the 1952 catalog by name and also as the *Ballerina Plaques*. They were made in the green and gold and also white and red (see page 104). Both sets were made with flesh color bisque. The catalog suggested using them, "...in combination with the popular ballet pictures, or a girl's room." More truth than fiction there. When my wife, Cindy, first saw the above pair she immediately recognized them as the ones that used to hang on the wall of her bedroom when she was a little girl. *Schneider Collection.*

Acknowledgments

I always feel a twinge of embarrassment when I see my name on the cover of a book because, although I am listed as the author, I know that if it were not for the numerous people who have unselfishly given of their time and allowed us to photograph their collections, each book I have written would amount to nothing more than a pair of covers with a lot of blank pages between them.

The first person I wish to thank for contributing to this book is Cindy, my wife, for her decision several years ago to collect Ceramic Arts Studio figurines. Seeing her collection day in and day out increased my appreciation of the company's work to the point that writing a book about it rose from passing thought to foregone conclusion.

But it was Betty and Floyd Carson who actually started both of us on the road that led to this project when they introduced us to Ceramic Arts Studio while we were shooting pictures for *Animal Figures*. Over the years, while photographing other books at their house, they always made available any Ceramic Arts Studio pieces they had recently picked up. Our thanks goes out to them not only for the pictures, but also for getting us started in a wonderful hobby.

Shirley and Dan King graciously allowed us to photograph their outstanding collection after we met them several times at flea markets and antique shows while engaging in the processes of buying and selling. As you will see, the pieces they have are absolutely wonderful.

While taking pictures of the King's collection, salt and pepper shaker collector Karen Weaver brought over several of her Ceramic Arts pieces which enabled us to broaden the scope of the book a bit more.

Richard and Susan Oravitz were again very helpful when it came to photographing their pieces. While their names do not appear in this book as often as they did in my last two, it's simply because they are very selective when choosing Ceramic Arts Studio figures to incorporate into their vast collection of mid-twentieth century American ceramics, which you will see much more of when my books on California figural pottery are published.

Good friends Allen and Michelle Naylor also supplied some pieces that we would otherwise had to have done without. Photographing their collections has become even more enjoyable since the arrival of Courtney a couple years ago.

Salt and pepper shaker collectors Irene & Jim Thornburg also contributed in that some of the pictures we took at their home for *The Complete Salt and Pepper Shaker Book* were reprinted for this one.

This picture shows two sets of salt and pepper shakers. The set in the middle is *Suzette on Pillow*. *Suzette* is 3 1/4 inches high, the *Pillow* is 2 3/4 inches across. Mark of the *Pillow* is shown. The other set is *Fifi* and *Fufu*. *Fifi*, on the left, was not measured. *Fufu*, on the right, is 2 3/4 inches high. Both are marked and named. *Thornburg Collection.*

Author's Note

In order to maintain as accurate a record as possible of the products of Ceramic Arts Studio, two different type styles have been used to specify the names of individual pieces. Those in *italics* represent the name that was actually used by the company. These were taken from three sources, the pottery's 1952 and 1954 catalogs, and the bottoms of the pieces themselves.

Names that appear in regular type are either rooted in previous author's writings, or have come from the jargon that has sprung up within the hobby. It should be noted that I used only the information I had in front of me, so names appearing in regular type may indeed be the ones that were used by Ceramic Arts Studio. Other writers might have had access to a larger number of catalogs, or may have found some pieces marked that I found unmarked, which is a rather common occurrence.

Collectors would benefit by disciplining themselves to use the italicized names exclusively when describing those pieces, that is, *Suzette on Pillow* instead of dog on pillow, poodle on pillow, etc. It is not a foolproof system of avoiding confusion because there are a limited number of instances where different pieces have the same names. But it would eliminate a good 90 percent of the confusion, which seems like a worthwhile goal.

Mark of *Suzette on Pillow*.

This is *Becky*, a head vase that stands 5 1/2 inches high and carries a Ceramic Arts Studio mark that includes the name. *Becky* is one of only two (the other is *Mei-Ling*) Ceramic Arts head vases that is not known to have a mate. *Schneider Collection.*

Contents

SECTION I: Collecting

Too many people confuse the words accumulating and collecting. Accumulating is simply going out and buying everything you find that falls within the limits of a specific type of collectible. Collecting, on the other hand, is a much deeper pursuit. Among other things, it involves knowing something about the companies and people who made the things you collect, how to positively identify them, and how to care for them. It also includes knowing how to assign realistic values to specific pieces, how to tell the authentic from the fake, and knowing where and how to satisfy your thirst for more information. All of those subjects are covered in the chapters of this section.

Chapter 1: History

Ceramic Arts Studio, of Madison, Wisconsin, began in either the very late 1930s or very early 1940s, depending upon which of several research sources you choose to believe. It lasted until 1955. For our purposes the starting date is not all that important

While the earliest Ceramic Arts Studio figurines exhibited fine mold detail, they were finished in rather boring solid color pastel pink, yellow, or blue glazes, or a clear glaze which made the objects white. This unmarked turtle, 2 3/8 x 4 inches, is a typical example. While I am a devoted Ceramic Arts Studio fan I'm afraid I have to admit that if I saw this turtle at a show and didn't know who made it, I would be hard pressed to pay more than 25 or 50 cents for it, if I wanted it at all. As a Ceramic Arts piece, however, it displays Betty Harrington's early talent as a designer, and serves as a precursor of the wonderful pieces she would eventually turn out. Nearly all of the pastel figures, incidentally, were marketed throughout the life of the company, according to Sabra Olson Laumbach in Harrington Figurines, so they must have remained popular with consumers. Laumbach states that later examples may be found with more detailed glazing. *King Collection.*

because this book deals with a somewhat shorter period, 1942 to 1955, the years during which the pottery focused on the production of slipcast figurines instead of its initial hand-thrown decorative wares.

Although his tenure with the company was apparently short-lived, the enterprise was started by a young man named Lawrence Rabbitt. A University of Wisconsin student pursuing a degree in art, Rabbitt, at the time, was working on a research project aimed at testing the potting characteristics of locally mined Wisconsin clays. Apparently impressed with what he saw, the young student decided to set up a pottery that used Wisconsin clays exclusively.

Before long Rabbitt was joined by Rueben Sand, a law student whose financial situation and business acumen complemented Rabbitt's artistic talent. Rabbitt spun out the pots, Sand marketed them. But the pair quickly discovered that making hand-thrown pottery was not only time consuming, but also that the results were erratic at best, so experiments with slipcast pieces began almost immediately. That's when Betty Harrington, the designer and modeler whose work and influence much of this book is about, entered the picture.

A secretary employed by the state of Wisconsin, Harrington had made a figure of a kneeling nude woman with some clay her young daughters had given her. Early in 1942 she took the figure to the fledgling Ceramic Arts Studio to see about the possibility of getting it glazed and fired. Sand not only accommodated her, he asked her to model additional figures for him. That began a relationship which lasted throughout the life of the business, a relationship from which today's collectors are still reaping the benefits.

While other modelers worked for Ceramic Arts Studio, it is generally acknowledged that Harrington was the creative genius behind the company's success. Of the more than 800 different pieces known to have been produced, Harrington designed more than half. And, when you look at most of the rest, it becomes obvious that she exerted strong influence over the work of other designers who were employed at the pottery. If it didn't match Harrington's style or, at the very least meet her approval, for the most part it wasn't produced.

Harrington worked part-time without pay the first year, then became a full-time paid employee and eventually shared in a percentage of the profits. She also became the organization's chief goodwill ambassador by setting up and working booths at trade shows, and by drafting letters to accompany cata-

logs that told how to work Ceramic Arts Studio's products into everyone's decor.

But much of Ceramic Arts Studio's success must be attributed to the outbreak of World War II. Our country's entry into it in 1941 left gift ware buyers scrambling to fill their shelves as their previously well-used Oriental and European supply lines simply ceased to exist. The hostilities opened the door for successful upstart pottery ventures in America, which, until then, were nearly always doomed to failure due to higher production costs than foreign operations.

It was also World War II that caused Ceramic Arts Studio's demise. Left with its industrial base in ruin, Japan focused on ceramics at the beginning of its rebuilding process. Japanese imports, while not nearly of the quality of American ceramics, found favor with the public due to their lower prices. The situation for our potteries steadily deteriorated during the American occupation from 1945 to 1952, then got worse after we left. Faced with rapidly diminishing sales and even more rapidly diminishing profits, Ceramic Arts Studio closed up shop in Madison in 1955.

According to BA Wellman in his *Ceramic Arts Studio Price Guide, 1992-93*, the *Paul Bunyan* plate is one of only two mass produced objects made at Ceramic Arts Studio prior to designer Betty Harrington's tenure with the company. The other is a 7 1/2 inch high pitcher and bowl set of which, unfortunately, I did not obtain a picture. The plate is 5 3/8 inches in diameter. Its mark is shown at right. *King Collection.*

Mark of the above *Paul Bunyan* plate. The two lines in the center which may be a bit hard to read say, "Wisconsin / Clays." Note that the bisque is similar in color to that of another fine upper Midwest pottery, Rosemeade.

My assumption is that these two examples of the stylized hen, complete with simple glazing in three colors, came pretty close on the heels of most of the solid color pastel figures such as the turtle. The hens are 3 3/8 inches high, unmarked. Their mates, of course, would be stylized roosters in the same color schemes. Laumbach shows a picture of the stylized rooster, which appears to be about an inch taller than the hen. Its neck goes straight up and down, and with its head tilted back slightly it appears to be crowing. In addition to a larger comb (five segments instead of four), the rooster carries a wattle under its chin, and its tail curves toward the ground and up its legs forming a hole in the figure. *Schneider Collection.*

From the humble beginnings shown above Betty Harrington and Ceramic Arts Studio went on to produce some of the finest figurines ever made in America, including this Mexican couple made of flesh color bisque. Unnamed, he stands 7 inches high, she 6 1/2 inches. Both have Betty Harrington/Ceramic Arts Studio marks. *Schneider Collection.*

This is *Frisky Baby Lamb*, according to the 1952 catalog, complete with the pink cheeks for which Ceramic Arts Studio is so well known. *Frisky* is 2 7/8 inches high, and is not marked. *Schneider Collection.*

Chapter 2: Identification

The best way to identify any figurine, including those made by Ceramic Arts Studio, is by a mark on its base, as shown below on the cat, *Boo,* on page 11. Unfortunately, many of the company's pieces had bases that were too small to mark. And, for whatever reason, a lot that did have bases large enough to mark were not marked.

So let's go to the second best way. That would be by familiarizing yourself with the pictures in this book, or by carrying it with you when you go shopping, to make on-site comparisons. That's not always possible, of course. And not all of the company's output appears in the book, anyway. On to the third best way.

That would be learning to recognize specific features many Ceramic Arts figures have in common, the telltale signs that will eventually enable you to purchase unmarked figures with confidence.

Number one would have to be the pink-glazed cheeks prevalent on many of the people figures and even on some of the animals. They are so much an identifying feature that a few years ago, before people like Sabra Olson Laumbach and BA Wellman began educating the public about Ceramic Arts Studio through the print and video media, some folks who had been collecting for years referred to their collections simply as rosy cheek figures. While other companies sometimes used this feature, once you be-come halfway familiar with Ceramic Arts Studio you will be able to tell the difference immediately.

Eyes are another clue. Compare the eyes in the close ups below of the faces of Lu-Tang and *Friskie Baby Lamb* and you will see they are very similar. Granted, there are differences, but the similarity is unmistakable. Ditto for most Ceramic Arts Studio pieces.

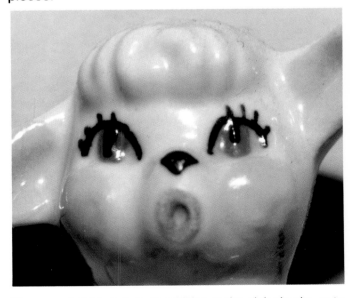

Close up of *Frisky's* face. In addition to the pink cheeks, note how the eyes--especially the lashes--are similar to Lu-Tang's.

And don't forget color. At first glance a collection of Ceramic Arts Studio figures looks like a glorious rainbow made up of a thousand different hues. But closer inspection will reveal the company actually used a rather limited number of colors. Make it a point to become intimately familiar with each of them.

Sometimes a name was printed on the bottom instead of a mark. That's the case with *Peek*, shown below. While *Peek* has just the name, its mate, *Boo*, was made with a larger base that allowed room for the name plus a mark. Other times just a copyright symbol was put on small pieces.

Detailed hand painting (actually hand glazing), is also a good clue. Check out the dots on the vest of *Colonel Jackson* (page 13), the flowers on the dress of *Miss Lucindy*, and the close ups of the detail on the Mexican lady. Although Ceramic Arts Studio's decorators were paid on a piece-work basis, the company obviously did not allow them to sacrifice quality in the name of speed.

Speaking of decorators, an interesting passage in Laumbach's book, *Harrington Figurines*, states that Ceramic Arts Studio preferred to hire decorators who had no background in art. According to Laumbach, amateur and professional artists, and former decorators, could not easily be convinced to decorate in Ceramic Arts Studio's style and apparently often had to be let go. The company gave hands on aptitude tests to unemployed people from all walks of life-- everyone from housewives to truck drivers--to build a competent decorating team.

Most of what are usually referred to as bisque face figures, such as *Zor* and *Zorina* (page 14), have common facial characteristics that you will know very well after acquiring just one pair, or for that matter, only one of a pair.

Sometimes colored bisque will provide the tell-tale clue necessary to positively identify a piece. The Mexican lady shown on page 13 was made with flesh color bisque. Other colors used include dark brown, pink, and one that comes very close to the color of yellow ware. By and large, however, the great majority of figures were made with common white bisque. After you become very familiar with Ceramic Arts Studio's products your sense of touch will further help you identify them. The glazes and modelling characteristics have unique feels to them. There's little doubt that after collecting for awhile you will be able to tell the difference between, say, a Goebel or Royal Doulton figurine, and a Ceramic Arts Studio figurine—blindfolded!

Closely related to touch is weight. Overall, Ceramic Arts Studio figures are fairly heavy when compared to Oriental imports of the same era. And many times, the smaller the base the heavier the figurine.

Consider the *Southern Couple*, page 13. As you can see, *Miss Lucindy* is larger overall and should be heavier. Not so. *Colonel Jackson* was poured heavier (left in the mold longer), apparently for stability. The same is true of other similarly shaped couples such as the *Gay 90s Man* and *Woman* shown in Chapter 8.

While all of the above hints will help you most of the time, there are some cases where familiarity is

According to Laumbach, this figure is named Lu-Tang although I have not found one with the name on it, nor does it appear in the 1952 or 1954 catalog. Her pink cheeks may be a bit hard to see in this picture, but there is no doubt in the close up below. Lu-Tang stands 6 3/8 inches high, has a Betty Harrington/Ceramic Arts Studio inkstamp. In Chapter 17: Planters and Vases she appears with her partner, Wing-Sang, on the bamboo bud vases. *Schneider Collection.*

the only answer. For instance, if you did not see a picture of the stylized deer,(page 14) prior to seeing them in person, you would probably not recognize them as Ceramic Arts Studio pieces because they are so out of line with what would be considered the company's normal style. The same goes for other pieces such as the *African Plaques* shown in Chapter 17.

But this problem is not insurmountable, nor is it very common. To give you an example I will relate my own experience. My first knowledge of Ceramic Arts Studio came about five years ago when writing my book, *Animal Figures*. For the past three years my wife has been what you would have to call an avid collector. I also gained considerable additional knowledge by photographing a couple large collections for this book, and for *The Complete Salt and Pepper Shaker Book*. Consequently, I consider myself to be very familiar with what a Ceramic Arts Studio piece should look like. Yet in the past year I have been fooled twice.

The first time was my friend Allen Naylor presented me with the stylized hens shown in Chapter 1. I'm sure, mainly due to their simplicity, that I never would have recognized them on my own. The second time was with *Honey* (page 14), who is shown with her companion, *Sonny*. I don't know what I was expecting when I picked up Honey and turned her over, but do know I was flabbergasted to find her Ceramic Arts Studio mark. And therein lies the key to the problem of missing out on Ceramic Arts Studio pieces you don't recognize--pick up and turn over every piece you see that exhibits quality on a par with the figurines you are seeking.

Peek and *Boo*, a pair of playful cats who have vastly different marks as shown below. *Peek*, the taller of this pair, stands 4 inches high while *Boo* is 2 3/4 inches. *Schneider Collection.*

Peek and *Boo* separated.

As you can see, *Boo* carries a typical Ceramic Arts Studio mark along with his or her name because the base is large enough to allow it.

Close up of Lu-Tang that leaves no doubt about her pink cheeks.

Different story on *Peek's* mark, only room for the name on the bottom of the front feet. A copyright symbol may appear on one of *Peek's* rear feet on some examples, as there appears to be enough room to have accommodated it.

Now that I have set myself up to be a seldom fooled expert on Ceramic Arts Studio, let me tell what happened a couple weeks after writing the above two paragraphs. I was sitting at the kitchen table one evening going through Laumbach's book, checking off figures I had pictures of for this book. When I turned to page 19 my eyes went immediately to the pink squirrel shown on page 14, after which I shot upstairs to my animal figures room at a speed that must have approached the sound barrier. There was the squirrel, *Squeaky*, sitting on a shelf somewhat lost in a menagerie of other solid color animals. I had bought it the week before at a flea market for $0.50, mainly because I thought someone had done some pretty nice work modelling the tail, the beads, and the overall pose. I remember thinking at the time that it might

have been made by one of the Morton potteries of Morton, Illinois. Or perhaps Brush. Or maybe McCoy. But Ceramic Arts Studio never entered my mind. Nor did it enter Cindy's mind when I showed the piece to her and she gave me that ho-hum look with which I have become so familiar over the past 16 years. Roughly translated it says: As long as *you* like it I guess it will be o.k. Now, of course, she has decided she likes the squirrel, too, and it has been permanently moved from my animal figures room to the living room where she keeps all of her Ceramic Arts Studio animals.

That said, I think I will head up to the bathroom, take a hot soapy washcloth and wipe every last bit of egg off of my face.

While a view of several Ceramic Arts Studio figures gives one the impression the pottery used many different colors, closer scrutiny will reveal that the same colors were used over and over again but often in varying amounts. In the picture above vivid orange appears in three of the figures as does light green (the stripes of the *Little Boy Blue* on the right are composed of dark blue and light green). Yellow comes into play four times. So does navy blue. Learn the colors of the glazes shown throughout this book and you will have gone a long ways toward being able to identify unmarked pieces.

Ceramic Arts Studio's decorators took great care to add detail to many pieces, the dots on the vest of *Colonel Jackson* and the flowers on the dress of *Miss Lucindy* being two examples. *Colonel Jackson* is 7 1/4 inches high, *Miss Lucindy* is 6 7/8 inches. Neither is marked. In addition to the above names, the 1954 catalog also referred to these figures as the *Southern Gentleman* and *Southern Belle*, collectively the *Southern Couple. Schneider Collection.*

The Mexican lady in a different color scheme than the one shown on page 8. Note the detail in the close-ups below. *Schneider Collection.*

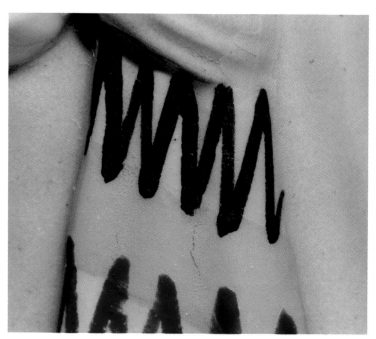

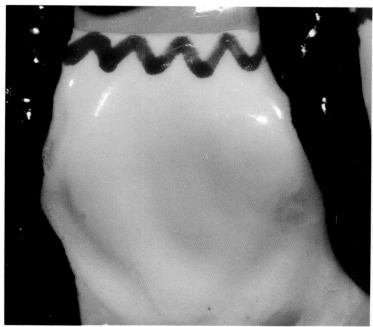

Detail of the Mexican lady's shawl. Note that it is all hand done. No decals for Ceramic Arts Studio.

Check out the precise decorating on the front of the Mexican lady; the rick-rack on her blouse goes just to the hem, there is absolutely no overlap on her braids.

Some Ceramic Arts Studio figurines were made of colored bisque as illustrated in this picture of the bottom of the Mexican lady. Other colors used in addition to white were yellow, pink and dark brown.

13

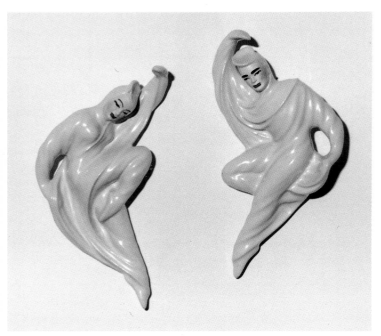

Some of the company's output had bisque faces, these wall plaques of *Zor* and *Zorina* being two examples. Once you see one and familiarize yourself with it you will be able to easily spot them from a distance. Both *Zor* and *Zorina* are 9 inches long. Both are marked and named. *Schneider Collection.*

When I picked up a tan and white *Honey* at an antique show and turned her over to find out who made her, I expected to see the word California printed somewhere on the bottom. Finding the Ceramic Arts Studio mark was a complete surprise. And that was after Cindy had been collecting Ceramic Arts for about three years, and I had looked at and handled hundreds, if not thousands, of pieces. *Honey* (tan) and *Sonny* (black) are each 5 5/8 inches high and are, in fact, made from identical molds but finished differently. Both are marked. They appear in the company's 1952 catalog where credit for the design is given to Ruth Planter. *King Collection.*

Not everything Ceramic Arts Studio made looks like Ceramic Arts Studio made it. The stylized doe and fawn, for example, are about as far from typical as you can get, and the only way to recognize them is by already having seen them, or turning them over and looking at their marks. The doe is 3 3/4 inches high, the fawn 2 inches. Both have Ceramic Arts Studio marks. *King Collection.*

There is a saying among media types that goes something like this: When a dog bites a man it's not news, when a man bites a dog it is news. Applied to squirrels it might go: When a squirrel buries a nut it's not news, when a nut buries a squirrel it is news. In this case I'm the nut who buried the squirrel in my animal figures collection without realizing it was made by Ceramic Arts Studio. *Squeaky* stands 3 1/8 inches high, is not marked. *Schneider Collection.*

This is *Mop-Pi* and *Smi-Li*, possessors of the dreaded red paint that chips and comes off so easily. If the paint does chip or peel one option is to take it all off (nail polish remover does a superb job) and repaint the area. *Mop-Pi* is 6 inches high, *Smi-Li* 6 1/4 inches. Each is marked. *Schneider Collection.*

Chapter 3: Care, Repair and Preservation

Care of Ceramic Arts Studio figures is not complicated, but there are a few pitfalls of which you should be aware.

One is red. Red is the toughest glaze color with which any potter or pottery has to work. It's the glaze color from hell! Apply it too thin and it will fire grey. Apply it too thick and it will turn black upon firing. Not surprisingly, many potteries both past and present, Ceramic Arts Studio included, have made a habit of using red paint instead of red glaze. Less pieces are ruined, which improves a company's bottom line. But it doesn't help the purchaser at all. Paint is not hard and fast like glaze. It chips. It rubs off. It washes off. So when washing your Ceramic Arts Studio pieces that have red paint on them (you can feel the difference between paint and glaze, paint is generally not as smooth as glaze), use only tepid water, a mild detergent, and very light pressure. If the red is chipped at all, the best idea might be to wash the rest of the piece but leave the red alone. Another option is to remove the red entirely and repaint it. If you are a dealer, never use a red area to tape on a tag or apply a price sticker as it will often pull the paint off when removed.

For washing I've found two soap applicators to work best--a discarded soft toothbrush and a cattail.

Cattails are cylindrically-shaped sponges attached to short dowel rods, which give them the appearance of the prolific swamp plant for which they are named. They are sold at hobby ceramic shops. Having a large one and a small one is recommended. The reason I use these two devices is because I can keep a firm grip on the figure with a hand that doesn't become soapy, and slippery, as generally happens when using an ordinary kitchen sponge. Surer grip, less breakage. You also get into those little cracks and crannies more easily and more completely with a cattail or toothbrush than with a common sponge.

One other note about cleaning. Wherever you keep your Ceramic Arts Studio collection, over time it is going to get dirty from dust, cooking vapors and possibly tobacco smoke and air freshener. A locked room, or even a china cabinet, will not keep these things out over the long haul. The pieces are going to eventually get dirty. Period. While how often you clean them is totally up to you, I recommend that you do it infrequently. Perhaps a good cleaning every few years, preferably in conjunction with having to move them, like when you are repainting the room, putting up new wallpaper or laying down new carpeting. Normal dirt and dust do not show that much anyway, and there's no way around the fact that the more any collection is handled the greater the chance of damage occurring.

There are a couple things you can do to avoid damage while your Ceramic Arts Studio collection is on display. Cindy uses floral clay to anchor top heavy pieces to prevent them from tipping over. It's inexpensive, easy to use and does not dry out for many years. But there is a downside to it in that it doesn't stick a second time. Once a figure has been moved, the floral clay must be taken off the bottom, worked between the fingers, and reapplied. We have a formerly perfect but now mended Lu-Tang to attest to ·the consequences if this is not done.

Metal doll holders, such as those holding Valentine Boy Lover, Willing and Bashful, are more expensive but probably a safer way to go. They can usually be purchased at antique shows or doll shows.

Another good preventative is to not get too carried away with replacing all the paraphernalia needed to make your Ceramic Arts figurines look 100 percent authentic. For instance, The *Hunter* below is usually found without his gun barrel, and *St. George on Charger* (Chapter 12) is often without his lance. Making wood or wire replacements is a rather simple task, and, indeed, will make your pieces look better. But they will also form dangerous protuberances just waiting to be struck by your hand or another figurine when you are adding to, taking from, rearranging or showing off your collection. The choice is up to each individual collector.

When damage does occur, it can usually be repaired to a certain degree. The repair may not be good enough to make the piece worth as much as it was before it was damaged, but certainly it will be good enough that anyone you are showing your collection to will probably not notice unless you call their attention to it.

Small chips are easy to repaint. I prefer Testor's enamels and apply them to chips with the point of a toothpick, which for a five-thumbed person like myself allows greater accuracy than would the finest sable artist's brush. I mix the paints together on a white saucer, experiment until I get the correct color. Testor's red enamel is perfect for replacing the missing red paint referred to above.

Ceramic Arts Studio used a fairly hard and durable pottery for its figures. Quite often when they break they break cleanly enough that a little white glue, such as Elmer's Glue-All™, and a steady hand will put them back together well enough so that probably no one but you will be the wiser. Elmer's is not waterproof so if you immerse your figurines to wash them use a glue that is. Incidentally, clean breaks and easy repairability is exactly why many Ceramic Arts Studio collectors carry a magnifying glass or

loupe with them when shopping. Most collectors do not arbitrarily rule out any broken or repaired piece, especially if it is a rare one, but when they are purchased they can generally be had for much less money after calling a dealer's attention to the repair. Most often it's the head you will find has been broken off and been glued back on, or perhaps the legs or feet of a sitter.

To sum up this chapter in one long sentence, inspect thoroughly before purchasing, handle carefully, clean sparingly, repair chips with Testor's, breaks with Elmer's Glue-All™, and watch out for red.

My personal Ceramic Arts Studio cleaning kit. While the cattails look a bit ragged, I actually prefer them that way. After they have been used enough that they slide up and down the shaft, you can extend the sponge beyond the tip of the wood to maneuver it into tighter places, to get crooks and crannies really clean. The assortment of tumbled stones at the front are small chips you can purchase reasonably at most rock shops. They are perfect for the insides of planters and vases. When mixed with a small amount of detergent and water they can be swirled to clean the really hard to reach places. Goo Gone™ is a must for all pottery collectors to remove price sticker adhesive.

No matter where or how you display your collection it is going to get dirty. While how often it gets cleaned is a personal choice for each collector, the less frequently, the less accidental damage.

This is Al the *Hunter* and Kirby, his dog. Al is 7 1/4 inches high. His mark includes the word *Hunter*. Kirby measures 2 3/8 x 3 7/8 inches. He is not marked. While Al obviously looks better and more realistic with a barrel for his gun, that touch of realism, in my opinion, is just an accident waiting to happen. A small, thin, often unseen piece such as a gun barrel can easily be snagged or bumped when figures are moved. *Schneider Collection.*

Many Ceramic Arts Studio figurines are top heavy, a characteristic that can lead to disaster. An inexpensive way to prevent them from toppling is to apply floral clay to the bottoms. Just remember that if you move the figure you must remove the floral clay, rework and reapply it.

A better but more expensive option to prevent top heavy figures from falling over is to use doll stands. It's also a more permanent solution, and much handier in situations where the figures are being handled often, such as when you are showing them off to friends or selling them at an antique show. The unofficial names of these figures are Valentine Boy Lover, Willing and Bashful. All four pieces are marked. Only Willing (blonde) was measured; she stands 5 inches high. *Thornburg Collection.*

Two versions of the *Siamese Cat* and *Siamese Kitten*. As you can see, the pair on the left is made up of two shakers. The pair on the right is figurines. At one time the figurines were worth more, but now, again in my opinion, the shakers command the higher price. The *Siamese Cat* stands 4 1/4 inches high, the *Kitten* 3 1/4 inches. Both have Ceramic Arts Studio marks. *Schneider Collection.*

Chapter 4: Value

To arrive at prices I consulted BA Wellman's 1992-93 *Ceramic Arts Studio Price Guide*, Laumbach's *Harrington Figurines*, general price guides such as *Kovel's Antiques & Collectibles Price List* and *Schroeder's Antiques Price Guide*, and interviewed many collector's and dealers. Taking all of those things into account, I then combined them with personal experience and knowledge to arrive at the prices listed in the price guide, prices that represent what I believe a knowledgeable collector would pay a knowledgeable dealer at the time this book is published.

Which brings up another point. This is the first book to be written on Ceramic Arts Studio that will enjoy wide distribution. I expect its appearance will cause prices to escalate a little, as we have so often seen happen in the past when a new book on a particular collectible is published. Because books are generally revised only every so many years, I suggest purchasing Wellman's price guide each year as the best means of keeping abreast of the current market. Instructions on how to obtain the price guide are listed in the Appendix Sources.

Another thing worth mentioning is the value of salt and pepper shakers as opposed to figurines.

Many pieces were made both ways. In *Harrington Figurines*, Laumbach states that figurines are worth 10 percent more than salt and pepper shakers. When she wrote that, back around 1984, it was no doubt correct. But that was before the ten books that are currently available on salt and pepper shakers were written, and before the forming of The Novelty Salt and Pepper Shakers Club, which now boasts more than 1200 members. Most of those members, and most shaker collectors who are not members, would not consider purchasing a pair of Ceramic Arts Studio figurines to fill a void in their shaker collection, even if they were priced exceptionally low. Since there are many more shaker collectors than Ceramic Arts Studio collectors per se, salt and pepper shakers today, in my opinion, must be valued higher than figurines. It's the law of supply and demand. The situation could change back, of course, if Ceramic Arts Studio increases in popularity. Again, refer to BA Wellman's price guide on an annual basis to keep up with any changes the market may undergo.

The set of *Wee Elephants* on the right, made with pink bisque, is Ceramic Arts Studio and so marked. The set on the left, made of white bisque, is an imposter marked "Japan." Heights of the two sets are identical, 3 3/4 inches for the males, 3 1/4 inches for the females. Note that when they are turned correctly the trunks form an S & P, as can be seen on the white salt and the pink pepper. *Thornburg Collection.*

Chapter 5: Fakes and Reproductions

Many Ceramic Arts Studio pieces were copied, mostly by overseas potteries. The example shown above is but one of what amounts to a virtual multitude. Most of the copies, however, were poorly executed and are very easy to spot when familiarity is combined with a little common sense.

Fortunately, the United States requires importers to mark their goods with the country of origin and most importers obey this rule. Many look-alikes are betrayed by their Japan or Made in Japan inkstamps.

With unmarked pieces quality of decoration is often the main giveaway. Of the numerous copies I have personally seen, only a handful have exhibited decoration on a par with that of the original Ceramic Arts Studio of Madison, Wisconsin. While these few required very close inspection to determine that they were counterfeits, all of the others could be spotted anywhere from three feet to across the room. Sometimes it's the thinly applied glaze that gives them away. Other times it's that the colors are just not quite true. And still other times, perhaps most of the time, it's that the details appear to have been applied by someone whose hand could be called anything but steady.

Weight is also an important consideration when attempting to assess authenticity. Generally, the im-

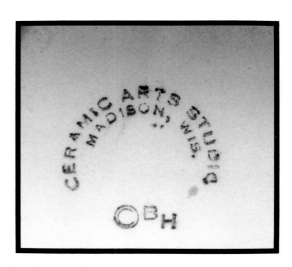

This is what is referred to often in the text as the "Betty Harrington/Ceramic Art Studio mark," the B.H. standing for Betty Harrington. This particular mark is from the Lorelei Planter shown in Chapter 17.

ported copies were poured much lighter than the originals. If you pick up a purported Ceramic Arts Studio piece and nearly bump the top of it against the bottom of the next shelf because it is much lighter than your subconscious mind told you it would be, it's best to set it down and move on. I have also seen some that are way too heavy, made of solid plaster instead of a fired pottery. To the best of my knowledge, Ceramic Arts Studio never worked with plaster.

Now to common sense. Most antique dealers I have met have been good honest people. As with anything else, however, once in awhile you do run into one who is not. If you happen to see a low priced Ceramic Arts Studio piece that doesn't look quite right in a display where all signs point to the fact that the dealer obviously knows a lot about the identification and value of American pottery, it would probably be best to forget about buying it. If it was genuine the dealer would have a higher price on it. A more common circumstance will be finding a look-alike represented as a genuine Ceramic Arts Studio piece because the dealer has made an honest mistake. Hopefully this will occur less frequently as this book makes its way into the hands of pottery dealers across the country.

So, while fakes and reproductions do exist, they really do not create much of a problem because they are generally very easy to spot. To those who are concerned about them because they are novices at collecting Ceramic Arts Studio, I would say don't be. Contrary to what you might think right now, your biggest surprise is not going to be how easily you got fooled, but how soon you were able to tell the difference.

A few years back the going price for this cat and pitcher was $5 to $10. Today Wellman shows it at almost $40, a good reason to purchase annual price guides. The cat stands 2 3/4 inches high and is marked. The pitcher measures 1 1/2 inches and is not marked. Laumbach shows the cat with a maroon pitcher. *King Collection*.

Chapter 6: Other Sources of Information

Information on Ceramic Arts Studio is scant when compared to other American potteries such as Brush, Rookwood or Shawnee. But what is out there complements this book in fine fashion, and I strongly urge you to take advantage of it.

Having read this far you are familiar, at least in name, with *Harrington Figurines*, by Sabra Olson Laumbach. This nearly all color book was published in 1985, and shows some of the pieces that are only named in this book. It has a very detailed history that goes beyond the scope of this simple identification and price guide, and also delves deeply into designer Betty Harrington's background and career. Among the treats waiting for you in *Harrington Figurines* are pictures of one-of-a-kind and "lunch hour" pieces including the original nude girl that brought Harrington and Ceramic Arts Studio together, pictures of Harrington's original sketches, Ceramic Arts Studio exhibit booths at trade shows, and work being accomplished within the pottery itself.

By now you have also been introduced to BA Wellman several times through the mentioning of his annual price guide. But Wellman also has several other offerings that will make you not only a better informed and more competent collector, but also a more fulfilled one.

His *Ceramic Arts Studio Video Books I & II* will bring both common and little known examples of this pottery's wares to your television screen. Rare pieces such as the adult band, Adam and Eve, and the Egyptian couple will parade across your living room, and you will also see a live interview with octogenarian Betty Harrington, and examples of her post-Ceramic Arts Studio work, some of which is quite fabulous.

Additionally, Wellman sells two Ceramic Arts Studio catalog reprints, both of which I relied on heavily when writing this book. One is from 1952, the other from 1954. As you might expect, they show examples you will not find here or in Laumbach's book.

The most recent source of additional information is the Ceramic Arts Studio Collectors Association. Formed in 1993, its purpose is to bring collectors together and spread information among them. Dues are $15.00 per year, for which you receive five copies of the newsletter, and free sell and want ads. Annual conventions are in the offing.

Information on how to obtain all of the above mentioned items can be found in Appendix Sources.

One last thing before we cut to the main feature. As you read this, I am already working on the *Ceramic Arts Studio Identification and Price Guide Volume II*. Readers who have Ceramic Arts Studio examples they would like to see included in it may send clear glossy 3 1/2" x 5" color prints along with the original negatives, plus size and mark information, to the author in care of the publisher. If requested, the materials will be returned after publication.

SECTION II: People–Present, Past and Around the World

Look at any representative collection of Ceramic Arts Studio figurines and you will quickly come to the conclusion that it was people figures that became the company's forte. From around the block to around the world, Betty Harrington, and perhaps other designers, portrayed children and adults in a certain style that captured the attention of gift ware buyers and consumers during the 1940s and 1950s, and has captivated many collectors today. There is probably no one reason for this popularity. Rather, it is a combination of factors--size, pose, facial expression, colors, decoration and others--which, when added together, resulted in a sum that equaled high quality people figurines at reasonable prices. That was no doubt true in the 1950s when a dozen *Jack* and *Jills* sold for $12 wholesale. And it is still true today as the modest prices of Ceramic Arts Studio pieces are dwarfed by those of Hummel, Royal Doulton, and other currently popular figurines.

Chapter 7: People in General

This chapter pictures people we see in everyday life. There is *Autumn Andy* on his way to school in the fall, a *Bride* and *Groom* exchanging their wedding vows, a *Summer Belle* decked out in her prettiest dress, to name a few. They are the people from your neighborhood and mine, the very commonly seen people we might often consider mundane, but whose differences make this world an interesting place to live. When placed together in a china cabinet, they will make your home an interesting place to visit.

While this pair is called *Jack* and *Jill* it seems doubtful that Ceramic Arts Studio had the famous nursery rhyme pair in mind when it named them as there is no pail of water, nor is anyone climbing up the hill or tumbling down it. Nor is the rhyme referred to in either the 1952 or 1954 catalog, both of which describe them simply as "...old fashioned children." *Jill* is 4 3/4 inches high, *Jack* is 4 7/8 inches. Neither is marked. *Schneider Collection.*

Jack and *Jill* in a different color scheme. *Schneider Collection.*

Another unnamed couple, the 1954 catalog calling them *Sitting Girl with Kitten* and *Sitting Boy with Dog*. They are not marked. At 3 5/8 inches, the girl is slightly smaller than the boy who is 4 inches. Note the two different colorways. The catalog said they came in assorted colors so there are probably several others. *Schneider Collection.*

A couple *Jills* in still different color schemes. *Schneider Collection.*

Although unnamed individually, the 1952 catalog referred to this pair collectively as the *Young Love Couple.* Each is 4 7/8 inches high. Each is marked. According to the catalog, they were also made in a blue color scheme. *Schneider Collection.*

Most collectors refer to this pair as the fishing boy and girl, but the 1952 catalog pegged them *Farmer Boy* and *Farmer Girl.* He is 4 3/4 inches high, she is 4 1/2 inches. Both have Betty Harrington/Ceramic Arts Studio marks. In addition to the green shown here, they were also marketed in blue. In order for the set to be complete you would have to have not only the *Farmer Boy's* fishing pole, but also the tiniest ceramic fish hanging from its thin line. Good luck. *Schneider Collection.*

Sitting Children, *Nip* and *Tuck*, according to the 1954 catalog. *Nip* (he) is 4 1/4 inches high, marked only by paper label. *Tuck* (she) is also 4 1/4 inches but unmarked. *King Collection.*

Jim and *June* in a different color scheme. *King Collection.*

Tuck in yellow. *Schneider Collection.*

Jim in still different colors. *Oravitz Collection.*

These are the *Standing Children Jim* and *June*. Heights are 4 1/4 and 4 1/8 inches, respectively. Neither is marked. *Schneider Collection.*

This cowboy and cowgirl are each 4 1/2 inches high. Both carry Betty Harrington/Ceramic Arts Studio marks. Note the tiny horse on each of their belt buckles and on the boy's chaps, which is shown close up below. *Schneider Collection.*

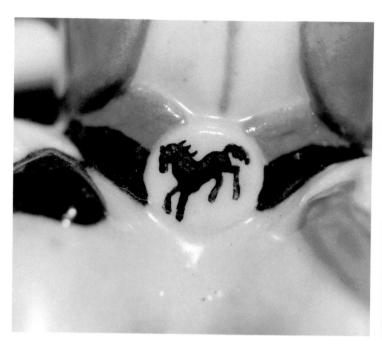

Horse on the belt buckle of the cowboy above.

The *Square Dance Couple Boy* and *Girl* are 6 3/8 and 6 1/8 inches high, respectively. They are not marked. The set was made in blue also. *Schneider Collection.*

Cowboy and cowgirl in a different color scheme. There may be several others. *King Collection.*

Called simply *Bedtime Boy* and *Girl* in Ceramic Art's 1952 catalog, he stands 4 1/2 inches high, she 5 inches. Each is marked. *King Collection.*

This picture shows two pair of salt and pepper shakers, the children and the chairs being individual pieces. The girl is 2 1/4 inches high when not kneeling on the chair. The boy was not measured. The chair? It stands 2 inches high with or without the weight of the children. All four pieces are marked. *Thornburg Collection.*

The *Clown* is 3 1/2 inches high, the *Clown Dog*, 2 inches. Both are marked. White and red is the only color scheme I have seen. *King Collection.*

The *Groom* of this handsome couple stands 4 7/8 inches high, the *Bride*, 4 3/4 inches. Neither is marked. This pair was advertised in Ceramic Arts Studio's 1954 catalog which suggested using them as a gift for the bride, a wedding cake topper, anniversary gift, or retail display. The catalog states they were made in three color combinations but does not say what they were. *Oravitz Collection.*

Summer Bell, one of three bells the company made. The other two, *Winter Bell* and *Lilibelle,* are shown below. *Summer Bell* is 5 1/4 inches high, unmarked. (It's not a typo; the company spelled the names of *Summer* and *Winter Bell* without an e on the end, *Lilibelle* with the e.) *Schneider Collection.*

Summer Bell in yellow and green, also unmarked. According to the 1954 catalog, Summer and Winter Bell were made in an assortment of color combinations. Schneider Collection.

Lilibelle is the largest of the three bells, and also the hardest to find. The figure stands 6 3/4 inches high. Like the others, it is not marked. The bow in her hair, of course, is the ribbon that holds the clapper. Lilibelle came in blue, green and brown combinations, according to the 1954 catalog. King Collection.

Winter Bell in two colorways. The figure is 5 3/8 high. It is not marked. Look closely at these two and you will find the one on the left has a ribbon around her neck, the one on the right does not. The ribbon goes through a small hole in the neck (visible under the chin of the dark blue model), runs down the inside and holds the clapper, which, incidentally, is shaped like a bell. Quite often these bells are found without their ribbons or clappers. My personal opinion is that their absence does not lower the value. If you are a purist you can always tie on another length of ribbon. Another reason that it is not all that important is that if the tone of all those I have heard is any indication, Ceramic Arts Studio went much further in the pottery business than it ever would have gone in the music business. Schneider Collection.

Lilibelle with brown hair. Schneider Collection.

Here are *The Four Seasons* as seen through the eyes of Ceramic Arts Studio: *Spring Sue, Summer Sally, Autumn Andy* and *Winter Willie*. Heights left to right are 5 1/8, 3 3/8, 5 1/8 and 4 inches. None of the pieces are marked. *King Collection.*

Two different *Autumn Andys.* The green substance beneath the soles of the shoes on the example on the left is floral clay. *Schneider Collection.*

Spring Sue in yellow. *Schneider Collection.*

Winter Willie in blue. *Oravitz Collection.*

Ceramic Arts Studio's 1952 Catalog calls this pair the *Colonial Sitting Pair Boy* and *Girl*. With the white hair I would be more inclined to call them man and woman. He is 5 inches high, she is 5 1/2 inches. Each is marked. According to the catalog, these were also made in yellow-green. *King Collection.*

Chapter 8: Historically Costumed People

Here is a short but beautifully illustrated time line of American fashion running from the Colonial period to the end of the Victorian era. Some of the figures shown below, the *Southern Couple*, for example, are fairly easy to find. Others, for instance the *Colonial Couple*, are somewhat harder to come by.

This is the *Colonial Couple Man* and *Woman*, 6 3/4 and 6 5/8 inches high, respectively. Neither is marked. They were made in several color combinations. *King Collection.*

Now comes the *Colonial Boy* and *Girl*, which were made, according to the company, to answer the demand for smaller colonial figures. Heights are 5 3/4 and 5 inches. Neither is marked, and they were made in several color combinations. *Oravitz Collection.*

When I bought this guy at the Springfield (Ohio) Antique Show and Flea Market a couple years ago, I came back to our booth and told Cindy I had gotten her Tom Tom the Piper's Son (who "stole a pig and away he run.") Bad guess. It's actually *Pioneer Sam* and his significant other, *Pioneer Susie,* together known as the *Pioneer Couple.* She is 5 1/8 inches high while he stands 5 5/8 inches. Neither is marked. *Schneider Collection.*

Pioneer Susie in solid blue. Another difference, too: she's marked. "The Ceramic Arts Studio / Madison / Wisc. / BH / Pioneer Susie" is incised on five lines. *King Collection.*

Pioneer Susie in a different color scheme. To be complete, *Pioneer Susie* would have to be holding her broom--a wooden or metal accessory--in her right hand. *Oravitz Collection.*

The *Southern Couple, Colonel Jackson* and *Miss Lucindy.* Heights are 7 1/4 and 6 7/8 inches, respectively. Neither is marked. Another color combination for this couple is shown on page 13. *Schneider Collection.*

Miss Lucindy in teal and blue, also unmarked. *Schneider Collection.*

Original *Gay Ninety Couple* in the blue color scheme, the only other available in the 1952 catalog. *King Collection.*

Here is the first of two versions of the *Gay Ninety Couple,* called the *Gay Ninety Man* and *Gay Ninety Woman* by the company. He is 6 3/4 inches high, she is 6 1/2 inches. Both have Betty Harrington/Ceramic Arts Studio marks. This pair appeared in the 1952 catalog. *Schneider Collection.*

Skip ahead to the 1954 catalog and we find a different *Gay Ninety Couple,* this time with names, *Harry* and *Lillibeth.* Heights are 6 1/2 inches for him, 6 3/8 inches for her. *Schneider Collection.*

31

Harry and *Lillibeth* in brown and yellow. *King Collection.*

The *Promenade Man* is 7 3/4 inches high, the *Promenade Lady* 8 1/8 inches. Both have Ceramic Arts Studio marks. Wellman shows the couple in rust. *King Collection.*

Three different *Lillibeths.* The two on the right are not marked. The one on the left is incised, "The Ceramic / Arts Studio / Madison / Wisc / BH / Gay 90s" on six lines. *King Collection.*

After looking over the above picture I realized I did a pretty poor job of showing you anything about the *Promenade Lady,* so here she is again with a few more details visible.

This is what is commonly referred to by collectors as the American Indian group--Hiawatha, Minnehaha, *Wee Indian Boy* and *Girl,* canoe planter, *Fawn, Bunny* and *Chipmunk.* Missing from the picture is the gull that sits on the edge of the canoe. Whether or not Ceramic Arts intended the animals to be in this grouping is a question of some debate. While they appear on the same page as the *Wee Indians* in the 1952 catalog, no mention is made of them having anything in common with each other, and the fact that the *Bunny* was also made in a white and pink combination casts additional doubt. Because this is an important grouping the figures are dealt with individually below and in Chapter 13: Mammals. Incidentally, all of the pieces in this picture except the canoe are made of flesh color bisque. *King Collection.*

Chapter 9: Ethnic Attire

People of many European countries, the countries of Asia and the continent of Africa sprang to life as a combination of clay and glaze inside the walls of Ceramic Arts Studio 50 years ago. Most were made with the rosy cheeks mentioned in Chapter 2, some with bisque faces, all with care, precision and skill.

Minnehaha, on the left, stands 6 1/2 inches high. Hiawatha is 4 3/4 inches. Both have Betty Harrington/Ceramic Arts Studio marks. Note that this set apparently was made in at least three different colorways as Hiawatha has blue trim, Minnehaha chartreuse, and the *Wee Indians* yellow. *King Collection.*

The canoe planter is 7 7/8 inches long, carries a Ceramic Arts Studio mark. The *Wee Indian Girl,* at 3 1/4 inches, is slightly taller than the *Wee Indian Boy,* who is 3 inches high. Each is marked with the Betty Harrington/Ceramic Arts Studio inkstamp. *King Collection.*

Bearing a close resemblance to the *Wee Indian Boy* and *Girl* is the *Wee Eskimo Boy* and *Girl.* The boy is 3 3/8 inches high, the girl 3 1/8 inches. Both are marked and both are made of flesh color bisque. *Weaver Collection.*

Hans and *Katinka* in green. Possibly a different mold for *Hans*, too, as my notes show him being only 5 3/4 inches. While a measuring error on my part is not out of the question, these two do appear to be closer to the same height than the pair below. Another difference here is that although *Hans* is still unmarked, *Katinka* does have a mark. *King Collection.*

This is the dancing *Dutch Couple, Hans* and *Katinka. Hans* measures in at 6 1/8 inches, *Katinka* at 5 3/8. Neither is marked. *Schneider Collection.*

Hans and *Katinka* in yellow. *Schneider Collection.*

Here's *Hans* and *Katrinka;* note the addition of the r in her name. While the omission of the r in the 1954 catalog description of the dancing pair at left may have been a typo, I decided to go with it to differentiate between the two sets. *Hans* is 6 1/2 inches high, *Katrinka* 6 1/4 inches. Both are marked. *Hans* is holding a bouquet of flowers behind his back. *King Collection.*

Katrinka in blue. According to the 1952 catalog, this set also came in green. *Schneider Collection.*

This is the *Dutch Love Boy* and *Dutch Love Girl,* each 4 7/8 inches high and unmarked. *Schneider Collection.*

The *Sitting Dutch Girl* measures 4 3/8 inches, the *Sitting Dutch Boy,* 4 1/4 inches. Each has a Betty Harrington/Ceramic Arts Studio mark. *Oravitz Collection.*

The *Dutch Love Couple* in yellow. At the time the 1954 catalog was printed, yellow and blue were the only colors in which this set was made. Of course, that doesn't necessarily mean it wasn't made in other colors during previous years. *King Collection.*

Everything the same as above but chartouse instead of blue. Note the hand-painted tulips on the girl's apron and the boy's neck scarf on these pieces. The same design also appears on the top of the boy's hat and on the back of the girl's. *Schneider Collection.*

Wee Dutch Boy and Girl, 3 and 2 7/8 inches high, respectively. Both are marked. *Schneider Collection.*

Same set, same marks, different color. *Schneider Collection.*

This pair was called *Big Dutch Boy* and *Girl* in both the 1952 and 1954 catalogs. She stands 3 3/4 inches high, he was not measured. Both have Betty Harrington/Ceramic Arts Studio marks. *Thornburg Collection.*

Like so many others, the 1952 catalog had very simple names for these two, *Chinese Boy* and *Chinese Girl*. Heights are 4 1/4 and 4 1/8 inches. Each is marked. According to the catalog, this is the only color scheme in which they were made. *Schneider Collection.*

That's it for Holland, now we're off to China. The *Chinese Sitting Boy* and *Girl* are each 4 inches high, and both are marked with the Betty Harrington/Ceramic Arts Studio inkstamp. *Schneider Collection.*

An unmarked *Chinese Couple, Ting-A-Ling* and *Sung-Tu. Ting-A-Ling* is 5 1/2 inches high, while the culturally subservient *Sung-Tu* is 4 inches. *Schneider Collection.*

Fun with words here, this anagram couple being named *Sun-Li* and *Su-Lin* by their creators. The male half, *Sun-Li,* measures 6 inches while his female counterpart, *Su-Lin,* comes in at 5 1/2 inches. Both of these sitters are marked. According to the 1952 catalog, they were also made in a red and yellow combination. *Schneider Collection.*

The *Wee French Boy* and *Girl* are each 3 1/2 inches high. Each is marked. *Thornburg Collection.*

Manchu and *Lotus* in a different color scheme and absent their lanterns. Finding these without the lanterns is common, finding the lanterns separately is almost unheard of. Good places to look are jewelry cases holding dollhouse furniture or knick-knacks at antique shows and malls. *Schneider Collection.*

This is *Manchu* and *Lotus,* a popular pair of names with the folks at Ceramic Arts Studio as they are also used for a pair of head vases in Chapter 17 Planters and Vases. *Manchu* is 9 1/8 inches, *Lotus* 9 1/4 inches. Each has a Betty Harrington/Ceramic Arts Studio mark that includes the individual names. *King Collection.*

This is the *Swedish Lady* and *Swedish Man,* according to the printing on their bottoms which also includes normal Betty Harrington/Ceramic Arts Studio marks. She is 6 1/2 inches high, he 7 inches. This is one of the few Ceramic Arts pairs on which the bases are made to fit together as shown below. *King Collection.*

The *Wee Sweedish Boy,* on the far left, is 3 1/8 inches high. The *Wee Scotch Boy,* far right, is 3 1/2 inches. All four pieces are marked. *Thornburg Collection.*

Swedish Man and *Lady* together.

Boy and *Girl* stand 6 1/2 and 6 1/4 inches rked. The 1954 catalog states they "...sug-.." *Schneider Collection.*

The *Polish Girl* in blue, green and yellow. Like the polish pair above, she is not marked. *Schneider Collection.*

The *Shepherd and Shepherdess* both carr Studio marks plus their names. Heights inches, respectively. Finding them with th *King Collection.*

Petrov and Petrushka are the names of the *Russian Couple.* Unmarked, they stand 5 3/8 and 5 1/4 inches high. *Oravitz Collection.*

The *Russian Couple* in teal. Notice the difference in the detail between this couple and the dark blue couple--the arms and belt of the boy, the apron and vest of the girl. *King Collection.*

Most collectors I know call this pair the Spanish couple, but the 1952 catalog pegs them the *Rhumba Dancers Man* and *Lady.* He is 7 1/4 inches high, she 7 1/8 inches. Both are marked. *Thornburg Collection.*

Rhumba Dancers in the green and maroon color scheme, the only other one available in the 1952 catalog. *Schneider Collection.*

The *Gypsies, Gypsy Man* and *Gypsy Woman,* with heavy gold (note the violin). Made of flesh color bisque, each carries a Betty Harrington/Ceramic Arts Studio mark. Heights are 6 5/8 inches for him, 7 1/8 inches for her. They were also made in green, according to the catalog. *Schneider Collection.*

Although you nearly always see the *Rhumba Dancers* with gold trim this piece shows that the company obviously made some without it. *Schneider Collection.*

This is *Pepita,* the female member of the *Pan American Couple,* according to the 1954 catalog. *Pepita* stands 4 1/2 inches high, is not marked. *King Collection.*

Pepita with different decoration. *King Collection.*

Pepita's mate, *Pancho,* 4 1/4 inches, also unmarked. *King Collection.*

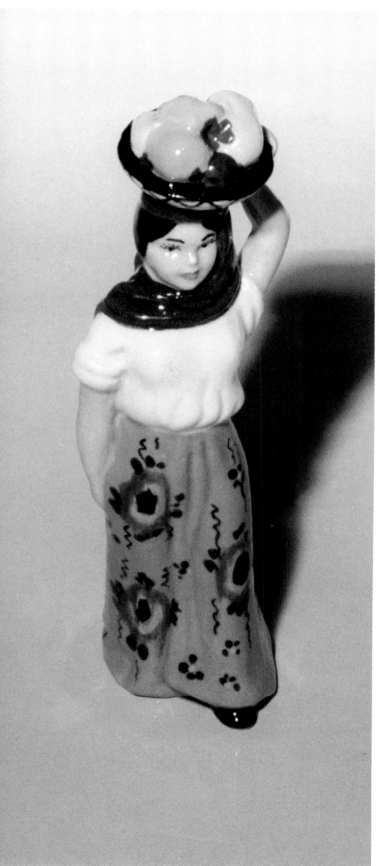

Carmen's companion, Carmalita, 4 1/4 inches high, unmarked. Schneider Collection.

Keeping with the Latino flavor, this is Carmen, the Cuban Woman of the Cuban Pair. Carmen is 7 inches high, unmarked. King Collection.

Carmalita in a different dress and with brown hair. King Collection.

Now it's on to Africa for the *Elephant* and *Boy,* as they were named in the 1952 catalog. The *Elephant* is 5 inches high, the *Boy* 2 3/4 inches. The *Elephant* is marked, the native *Boy* is not. My advice if you are lucky enough to own this pair is to fasten them together with Scotch Tape as the *Boy* is susceptible to falling off, a fact attested to by the large number of *Elephants* you see minus their riders. *King Collection.*

If you hear a fellow collector talking about the Hindu boys or Ethiopian palace guards, this is the set of which they are speaking. Since I prefer to stick to one common name I will call them the *Blackamoor* salt and pepper, which is how they were described in the 1954 catalog. Each is 4 3/4 inches high. Both have Ceramic Arts Studio marks. Note the P and S on their turbans. According to the catalog, this is the only color scheme in which they were made. *King Collection.*

The *Crocodile* is 4 5/8 inches long, the *Boy* is 2 1/2 inches high. The *Crocodile* is marked, the *Boy* is unmarked. This is another rare and highly desirable set you may choose to tape together. *King Collection.*

The backs of the *Blackamoors* are interesting in that they carry, at the very least, a suggestion of a P and an S, thereby making it possible for people sitting on the opposite side of the table to pick up the correct shaker should they want only one.

The 1952 catalog lists these as the *Balinese Dancers Man* and *Woman.* The *Man* stands 9 5/8 inches, the *Woman* 9 3/8 inches. Mark information was not recorded. According to the catalog, they were made in live green, cocoa brown and chartreuse color combinations. *King Collection.*

Bali-Hai and Bali-Gong. Bali-Hai stands 7 7/8 inches high, Bali-Gong 5 1/4 inches. Both are marked. *King Collection.*

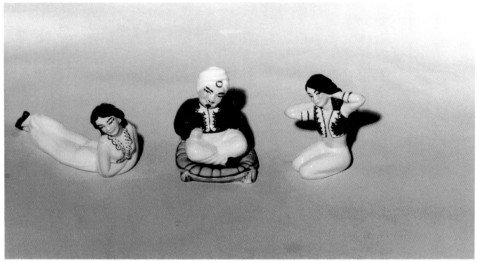

The *Harem Group* is made up of the *Harem Girl Reclining* 3 1/2 x 6 1/4 inches, the *Sultan* 4 3/4 inches high, and the *Harem Girl Sitting* 4 1/2 inches high. *King Collection.*

Sultan and *Harem Girl Sitting.* According to the 1952 catalog, predominating green and brown were the only colors in which these were offered. But considering that the *Harem Girl Reclining* in the above picture is wearing a yellow top with brown trim, I would not be too surprised if the green set appeared some day with the colors reversed. Another thing to keep in mind on these is that sometimes the *Sultan* is fused to the pillow, other times they are two separate pieces. *Thornburg Collection.*

Comedy and *Tragedy,* described in the 1952 catalog as "curvaceous dancers with lovely lines." I could not agree more. *Comedy,* on the left, stands 10 3/8 inches high. *Tragedy* measures in at 10 inches. Both are marked and named. *King Collection.*

Chapter 10: The Arts

Based on the number of these types of pieces the company made, the movers and shakers at Ceramic Arts Studio obviously had a fondness for the arts. However, it may be that that fondness was not shared by consumers as some of these figures are very hard to find. Size and cost may have had something to do with it, too. In the early 1950s Ceramic Arts Studio sold the *Frisky Baby Lamb* shown in Chapter 2 for as little as $7.20 per dozen wholesale, the *Sitting Dutch Couple* from Chapter 9 for $12 per dozen. Larger pieces, however, such as *Comedy* and *Tragedy* below, carried a wholesale price tag of $24 per dozen.

Here is the perfect reason to not accept as gospel the information printed in a limited number of specific year catalogs of any company. While the 1952 catalog refers to the green figures shown above, and also says they were made in chartreuse and burgundy, it makes no mention of this grey color. Grey may have been unsuccessfully tried at an earlier time and consequently dropped, or may have been added later, or who knows what. The catalog also does not refer to *Comedy* in black or *Tragedy* in white as Laumbach shows them. Marks and sizes are the same as above. *Schneider Collection.*

This is *Bruce* and *Beth,* both of whom are marked and named. *Bruce's* height is 6 1/4 inches, while *Beth's* is 4 3/4 inches. *Schneider Collection.*

Study this picture carefully because at first glance it looks a lot like *Bruce* and *Beth.* But it's actually *Dance Moderne Man* and *Dance Moderne Woman,* 9 7/8 and 9 1/4 inches, respectively. Mark information was not recorded. When you look at these pictures it's easy to tell the difference between *Bruce* and *Beth* and *Dance Moderne.* The problem comes when you are out searching at a flea market or antique show and don't have the book handy. I'm almost positive I passed up this pair one time because I thought they were *Bruce* and *Beth,* which Cindy already had. According to the catalog, they were also made in the color combinations of chartreuse and brown, and deep rose with grey. *King Collection.*

Shelf sitters *Maurice* and *Michelle,* 7 1/8 and 8 1/4 inches high, respectively. Each has a Ceramic Arts Studio mark along with its name. *Schneider Collection.*

Bruce and *Beth* in chartreuse, marked and named as above. *King Collection.*

50

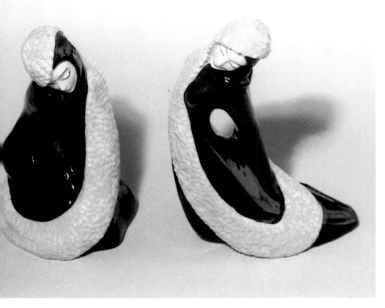

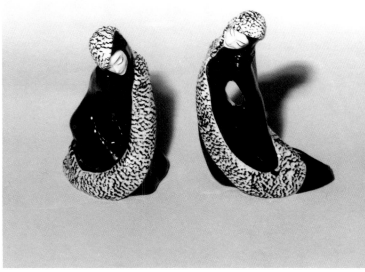

That's *Pensive* on the left, *Blythe* on the right. They are 6 and 6 1/2 inches high, marked with the normal Ceramic Arts Studio ink stamp plus their names. They do not appear in either the 1952 or 1954 catalog. *Oravitz Collection.*

Pensive and *Blythe* in a different color. Sizes and marks are the same as above. Laumbach, incidentally, shows this pair in rust and gold. I wonder how many other colors they may have been made in. *King Collection.*

These are some of the tallest Ceramic Arts Studio figurines of which I am aware, both measuring in at 11 1/2 inches. They are the King's Jester *Flutist* and King's Jester *Lutist*. Both are marked and named. About a year ago I passed this pair up--one perfect, one repaired--for $50, about half of the going price for just one of them. Haven't seen them for sale since and still cannot mention the incident around Cindy if I want to have a peaceful household. *King Collection.*

Like most parents, mine always said I should study hard in school and get as much education as possible. Perhaps if I had, I would recognize the significance of the *Water Man* and *Water Woman,* both of whom are marked and named, and who stand 11 1/4 and 11 1/2 inches, respectively. Like the *Fire Man* and *Fire Woman* below, they appear theatrical so I am tossing them in here. The 1952 catalog describes them as "Interpretive and understandable modern." It also states they were finished with a sea green glaze as well as the chartreuse shown. *King Collection.*

Fire Man and Fire Woman, 11 1/4 and 11 1/2 inches high. Each is marked and named. *Schneider Collection.*

Fire Man in grey, the only other color in which the set was offered in the 1952 catalog. *King Collection.*

Grace and *Greg* sitters as opposed to the *Grace* and *Greg* wall plaques shown in Chapter 18. *Grace* is 6 1/4 inches high, *Greg* 7 inches. Mark information was not recorded. *King Collection.*

On the left is *Ballet En Pose,* 5 1/4 inches high. *Ballet En Repose* is on the right, also 5 1/4 inches high. Each has a Betty Harrington/Ceramic Arts Studio mark along with its name. The 1952 catalog referred to them collectively as the *Ballerinas.* Besides lime green, these were also made in turquoise as shown by Laumbach. *Schneider Collection.*

This is *Rose,* 5 3/8 inches high, made of flesh color bisque and marked with the Ceramic Arts Studio inkstamp and her name. Note that she is named for the decoration that adorns her costume. *Schneider Collection.*

Like *Rose, Daisy* is also named for the flowers on her outfit. Bisque and mark are the same as above, height is 6 1/4 inches. There are two more members of this set that I was unable to photograph. *Pansy,* standing with her arms up and hands on her head, has a base identical to these two. *Violet,* on the other hand, is sitting with her right leg extended, her left leg drawn up with her hands around the ankle. Whether these were marketed as two pair, a set of four, or both, I do not know. *Schneider Collection.*

That's *Pierette* on the left, *Pierrot* on the right. Both are 6 3/4 inches high, both are marked and named. Note that *Pierette* sits as a man might while *Pierrot* poses more like a lady. *Schneider Collection.*

The *Bass Viol Boy* stands 4 3/4 inches high. Like all of these musician figurines I have seen, it is unmarked. *King Collection.*

This is what is commonly referred to by collectors as the eight-piece children's band, but according to the 1954 catalog, it is actually two separate sets or, more correctly, an original set with additions. According to the catalog, the *All Children's Orchestra* came first. It was composed of the *Guitar Boy, Bass Viol Boy, Flute Girl, Sax Boy* and *Drum Girl.* The *Musical Trio,* which the catalog refers to as, "An addition to our popular orchestra children," was made up of the *Accordion Boy, Harmonica Boy* and *Banjo Girl.* Each of the figurines in this group picture is also shown close up. *King Collection.*

Both the *Guitar Boy* and *Accordion Boy* are 5 inches high. Note that the colors are different than in the group photo. *Schneider Collection.*

The *Flute Girl*, 4 3/4 inches high. *King Collection.*

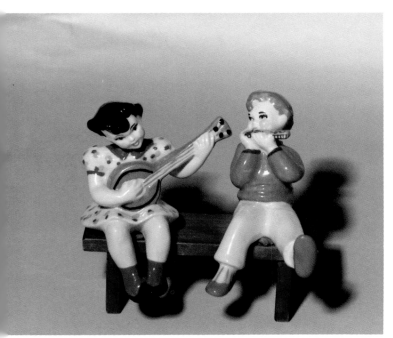

The *Banjo Girl* is 4 1/4 inches high, the *Harmonica Boy* 4 5/8 inches. The girl is a different color than that shown above. *Schneider Collection.*

The *Harmonica Boy* in green. *Schneider Collection.*

The *Sax Boy* is 5 1/8 inches high. *King Collection.*

The *Drum Girl* with blonde hair, 4 3/8 inches high. *Schneider Collection.*

This is one of two known Madonnas the company made. It is 5 3/4 inches high. Mark information was not recorded. Laumbach shows this one in airbrushed tan with hints of white, the same way she shows the other one, which is standing and about 10 inches high. *King Collection.*

Chapter 11: Religious Figures and Angels

Religious figures seemed to evade me when I was taking the photographs for the book. I think there are three possible reasons for that. One is that not many were made. Another is that a lot of them were accidentally broken and consequently discarded. A third and more likely reason, as I see it, is that these figures were purchased mainly by families in which religion was of major importance, and have been passed down from generation to generation, never coming back into general circulation through auctions or estate dispersals.

The other part of this chapter, angels, are not exceedingly common but are generally available if you search diligently for them. Speaking of angels, the small Japanese angels that were imported in huge numbers during the 1950s and 1960s, the ones that are commonly called angels of the month, birthday angels, etc., have become very collectible in the last couple years. Whenever you see a display of them in an antique shop or at a show, look closely to see if there might not be a Ceramic Arts Studio interloper hiding somewhere in the crowd.

A few more angels, on candleholders, appear in Chapter 19.

While this set of angels does not appear in either the 1952 or 1954 catalog, we know one thing about them for sure--they came in at least two different color schemes. Laumbach refers to them as angel praying and angel sleeping. The boy is 4 1/8 inches high, the girl 4 1/4 inches. Each is marked. *King Collection.*

On the left is *Angel Arm Down,* which goes with *Angel Arm Up* shown below. *Angel Arm Down,* 5 1/4 inches high, is unmarked. The unmarked piece on the right was not in either of the catalogs to which I had access. It is 5 inches high, and both Laumbach and Wellman call it angel with candle. Laumbach shows it in solid pink, Wellman refers to it as a single which it may well be. On page 71 of Laumbach's book, a picture of a Ceramic Arts Studio trade show exhibit shows angel with candle placed on a shelf between angel praying and angel sleeping. *King Collection.*

This angel is 6 1/2 inches high, has a Ceramic Arts Studio mark. Wellman calls it angel standing with a star, one of three pieces of what he refers to as the angels to the stars group. The other two pieces are angel praying on knees, and angel singing, which I assume to be the piece shown immediately below. *King Collection.*

Angel Arm Up, 6 1/2 inches high, unmarked. This particular example has had its hand glued back on so Cindy covered the flaw with the ribbon. Which points out something that should be remembered, that if you happen to run into a piece with a ribbon on it, it may pay to check underneath to make sure it's not covering a repair. Also be sure that price stickers are not covering chips or repairs before putting down your money. *Schneider Collection.*

Height of this seated singing angel is 3 5/8 inches. It has a Ceramic Arts Studio mark. I'll never forget buying this piece. The flea market vendor had $4 on it, I asked her if she could do any better. "No less than $3.50," she said. "A friend of mine told me this junk is collectible." Wouldn't most of our wallets be a lot thicker if all flea market dealers regarded this "collectible junk" as highly as that lady did. *Schneider Collection.*

Cinderella and her *Prince.* He stands 6 3/4 inches high, she
6 3/8 inches. Each has a Ceramic Arts Studio mark in addition
to the words *Cinderella* and *Prince. Schneider Collection.*

Chapter 12: Fiction, Verse and Legend

This could probably very easily be called the chapter of memories as it contains some of the characters from the stories and poems our mothers read to us when we were children, some from movies we have seen, and some from books we read when we were young, or perhaps when we weren't so young. *Hansel and Gretel, Little Miss Muffet, Cinderella,* even *St. George* and the dragon appear here. There is also that red-suited roly poly old gentleman who is undoubtedly every child's favorite--Santa Claus.

Not appearing is one of Ceramic Arts Studio's premiere sets, *Alice* and the *March Hare.* You will find it on the title page.

I wonder how many people would recognize *Cinderella* without the *Prince* if she had black hair as shown here. Heights and marks are the same as above. *Schneider Collection.*

This is *Wendy* and *Peter Pan*. Neither is marked, both are 5 1/2 inches high. According to the 1954 catalog, they were made in "assorted colors." Laumbach, for instance, shows *Peter Pan* with a blue vest. She also shows the leaves with more yellow in them. The characters are glazed to the bases. Wellman, however, states that the bases may be found separately, so perhaps the characters may be found separately, too. *King Collection.*

Hansel and Gretel in a different color scheme. Note that their hair colors are reversed. *Oravitz Collection.*

A one-piece, *Hansel and Gretel*, 4 1/4 inches high. This unmarked figurine was offered in the 1954 catalog. *King Collection.*

Sambo stands 3 1/4 inches high, is made of bisque the color of his skin. The tiger measures 2 5/8 x 5 1/4 inches. Both are marked but I have also seen them unmarked. *Weaver Collection.*

60

This picture shows two of the three children that go with the *Pied Piper and Children* set. On the left is the *Running Girl,* 2 7/8 inches high. On the right is the *Running Boy,* 2 3/4 inches high. Neither is marked. *King Collection.*

Ceramic Arts Studio made three sets of *Jack Horner* and *Miss Muffet.* According to Laumbach, this picture shows *Jack Horner no. 2* and *Miss Muffet no. 1,* while the picture immediately below shows *Miss Muffet no. 2.* According to the 1954 Catalog, the *Jack Horner* that goes with the *Miss Muffet* in this picture is a shelf sitter approximately 4 1/2 inches high, his pie held on his lap with his right hand, his left arm up in the air with a plum on his thumb. The *Jack Horner* shown here is 4 1/4 inches high, unmarked. This *Miss Muffet* is also 4 1/4 inches high, also unmarked. *King Collection.*

This is the third child that goes with the *Pied Piper and Children,* the *Praying Girl.* She's unmarked, 3 inches high. The *Pied Piper* himself was unavailable to photograph. He stands approximately 6 inches high and, of course, is blowing his horn. As you can see from these pictures, the set was made in several different colors. *King Collection.*

This is *Little Miss Muffet no. 2,* who obviously goes with the *Little Jack Horner* shown above. She is 4 1/2 inches high. Mark information was not recorded. Now for the third set. *Little Miss Muffet no. 3,* shown in Laumbach's book on page 59, is holding her curds and whey on her lap with her left hand, is waving with her right hand. *Little Jack Horner no. 3,* shown on the same page, is holding his pie in his right hand balancing it on his lap and against this stomach, his left arm is held at waist level and he has a plum on his thumb. *King Collection.*

Little Boy Blue is 5 3/8 inches long; all that I have seen have been unmarked. According to the 1952 catalog, he was also made in green. *Schneider Collection.*

The 1954 catalog shows this pair and calls them *Mary* and her *Little Lamb*. *Mary* is 6 inches high, the *Little Lamb* is 3 5/8 inches high. Neither is marked. *Schneider Collection.*

Little Bo Peep stands 5 1/4 inches high, all three are unmarked. While *Little Bo Peep* and *Little Boy Blue* are shown as a pair in both the 1952 and 1954 catalogs, in the 1952 edition they are priced separately. I believe that for the most part they must have been sold separately because although they are two of the most common Ceramic Arts Studio figurines, you very seldom see them being sold as a pair. *Schneider Collection.*

Mary in a different color, same size and unmarked. *Oravitz Collection.*

Paul Bunyan, 3 7/8 inches high. The tree stands 2 1/8 inches. *Paul Bunyan* has a paper label on his back that states his name. If you ever run into a duplicate of this set and you don't have the Santa Claus set immediately below, do not sell or trade the tree because it is the same one that goes with Santa Claus. *Weaver Collection.*

This is *St. George,* getting ready to kill the dragon and save *Lady Rowena.* His lance, which was an accessory piece of wood or metal, is missing. Height is 8 1/2 inches. The piece has a Ceramic Arts Studio mark along with the words *"St. George on Charger."* Schneider Collection.

Santa Claus is 2 inches high. Mark information was not recorded. *Thornburg Collection.*

Not surprisingly, the underside of this figure reads, *"Lady Rowena on Charger."* The figure is 8 1/4 inches high and has a Ceramic Arts Studio mark. According to Wellman, chargers were also made without riders. Note, too, that both chargers are exactly the same. *Schneider Collection.*

Here's the third member of the trio, *Archibald the Dragon,* as printed on its bottom. It also has a Ceramic Arts Studio mark, and stands 6 1/4 inches high. *Schneider Collection.*

Cupid stands 5 inches high, is not marked. Laumbach shows this figurine with a yellow base, wings and quiver, dark brown hair and quiver strap. *Schneider Collection.*

Archibald in green, and from a different angle. Size and marks are the same as above. Laumbach pictures *Archibald* in pink with black wings, *St. George* in yellow on a green charger. *King Collection.*

SECTION III: The Animal Kingdom

A lot more animals were made at Ceramic Arts Studio than many people realize. And they were made in great variety. Some of the animals such as the fighting leopards are very natural in design. Others, lions and deer, for example, were highly stylized and look little like their true counterparts seen in the wild. The third and last type we'll call cutsies. Included here would be the *Wee Piggys*, the turtle with monocle and top hat, and other similar critters.

This is *Fufu*, 2 3/4 inches high, unmarked. The other half of the pair is *Fifi*. Both are shown in white and pink on page 2. *King Collection.*

Chapter 13: Mammals

Ceramic Arts Studio made more mammals than any other kind of animal, probably because most people relate more to mammals than to birds, fish, reptiles, etc. All of the pottery's mammals that I have seen have been fully glazed. Most of them were made in pairs, a few were produced as singles.

The 1952 catalog calls the pair on the left *Sooty* and *Taffy,* and refers to them collectively as *Scotties.* Both are three inches high, each is marked. The pair on the right appear in the same catalog as *Pomeranian Pets, Pom Standing* and *Pom Sitting. Pom Standing* is 2 3/4 inches high, *Pom Sitting* is 2 inches. Both are unmarked but I have also seen them with marks. *Thornburg Collection.*

This is two figures, *Billy* and *Butch*. *Billy,* on the bottom, is 3 5/8 inches long. *Butch* is 3 inches high. Mark information was not recorded. They are shown separated below to give you a better idea of what they really look like. *Weaver Collection.*

The spaniel on the left stands 2 3/8 inches high. The pup on the right is 1 1/2 inches high. Both are marked. *Weaver Collection.*

Billy and *Butch* separated.

Spaniels in brown. *Weaver Collection.*

A one-piece pair of Scotties, 2 5/8 inches high. The figure is not marked. This was also made in black as shown below. *Carson Collection.*

This collie shelf sitter is 5 1/8 inches high and unmarked. The 1954 catalog called it the *Large Collie,* part of the *Collie Dog Family,* the rest of which is shown below. *Schneider Collection.*

Because it would take a much better photographer than me to get something recognizable out of the pure black faces of these Scotties, I decided to shoot them from the back to show the colorful detail of their bows. I imagine the bows were glazed in several different colors. Same size as above and unmarked. According to Laumbach, these Scotties were made exclusively for Montgomery & Wards which ordered more than 10,000 of them. *King Collection.*

Most of the rest of the family. As best as I have been able to tell, Ceramic Arts Studio made at least six different collie pups, the one missing from this picture being a four legged model. Sizes here, left to right, are 2 inches high, 2 1/2 inches long, 2 1/4 inches long, 2 1/2 inches long and 1 7/8 inches high. None of the pieces are marked. Take a close look at the pups on each side of the center pup. The one on the left of the center pup is called *Collie Pup Sleeping* (head straight), while the one on the right is called *Collie Pup Sleeping* (head turned). *King Collection.*

This is the *Sitting Cocker* and the *Standing Cocker.* Heights are 2 3/4 and 3 inches, respectively. They are not marked. *Schneider Collection.*

The dog is 1 1/2 inches high, the doghouse is 1 3/8 x 2 1/4 inches. Both are marked. They are shown separated below. *Thornburg Collection.*

The *Standing Cocker* in black and white, 2 3/4 inches high and unmarked. *Schneider Collection.*

Dog and doghouse separated. *King Collection.*

This puppy, 2 7/8 inches high, is unmarked but appears in Laumbach's book in a picture of a Ceramic Arts Studio trade show display. Its mate appears to be from the same mold but done in darker colors. *King Collection.*

This is the *Gingham Dog* and *Calico Cat* about which Eugene Field wrote. The cat stands 2 7/8 inches high, the dog 2 3/4 inches. Each is marked, each is made of yellow bisque. According to the 1952 catalog, this is the only color scheme in which they were made. *Schneider Collection.*

Thai and *Thai-Thai* as both salt and pepper shakers and figurines. That's *Thai-Thai* taking a snooze, *Thai* is the one with open eyes. *Thai-Thai* is 2 x 5 1/4 inches, Thai, 2 1/8 x 4 3/8. Both are marked and named. *King and Weaver Collections.*

The two parents of the *Persian Cat Family, Large Cat* on the left 5 1/2 inches high, *Tomcat* on the right, 5 inches high. (Heights include tails.) Each is marked. In the 1952 catalog, these are shown with the three kittens shown and described below. *Schneider Collection.*

In the 1954 catalog the kittens of the *Persian Cat Family* that are shown and described above have been replaced by these two and the one immediately below. *Sleeping Kitten,* on the left is 1 inch high and unmarked. *Washing kitten* on the right is also unmarked, 2 inches high. *Oravitz Collection.*

This kitten, *Kitten Washing,* is one of three that make up the rest of the *Persian Cat Family* in the 1952 catalog. The other two are *Kitten Playing* (faces left) and *Kitten Sleeping* (faces right).

Scratching Kitten, 1 7/8 inches high and unmarked, rounds out the 1954 rendition of the *Persian Cat Family. King Collection.*

This pair of stylized black cats do not appear in either of Wellman's catalog reprints. They are 4 1/4 and 2 1/4 inches high. Each is marked. *King and Weaver Collections.*

Tom Cat, 4 3/4 inches high, unmarked. The 1954 catalog says he may be used alone or as "the proud father for the cat family.' I assume that to mean the *Persian Cat Family* shown on page 70. *King Collection.*

Stylized cat in brown. *Schneider Collection.*

This cat was called both *Small Cat* and *Bright Eyes* by the company. It is 2 7/8 inches high, has a Ceramic Arts Studio mark. According to the catalogs, it was offered like this with blue or green highlights, or in the plain colors of pink or light blue. *King Collection.*

Both of the these horses are 6 inches high. The one on the left has a Ceramic Arts Studio mark along with the words *Fighting Stallion / Lightning* on two lines. Ditto for the one on the right but the name is *Thunder. Schneider Collection.*

Palomino Colt, 5 3/8 inches high, is unmarked. *Courtesy of Allen and Michelle Naylor.*

This is called *Balky Colt* in the 1952 catalog where it is shown with its mate, *Frisky Colt. Balky Colt* stands 3 5/8 inches high, unmarked. *Frisky* is approximately the same size. According to the catalog, the pair was also finished in a black and white color scheme. *Schneider Collection.*

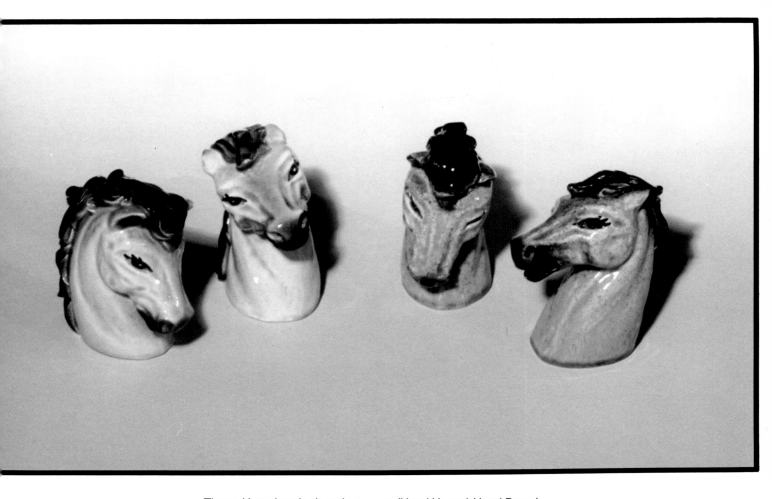

These *Horsehead* salt and peppers *(Head Up* and *Head Down)*
are 3 3/8 inches high. Each has a Ceramic Arts Studio mark.
Thornburg Collection.

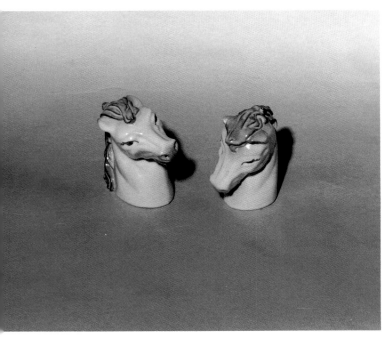

The *Horseheads* in white and grey. *Weaver Collection.*

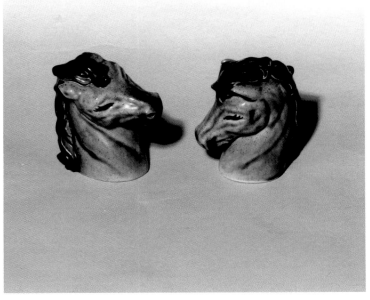

Horseheads in green. *Weaver Collection.*

The ox is 3 1/2 inches long, the wagon 2 3/8 inches high. Both are marked. *Thornburg Collection.*

Collectors call these the modern lambs. The one on the left is 2 inches high, the one on the right 2 1/2 inches. Each has a Ceramic Arts Studio mark. *King Collection.*

Modern lambs in maroon. Laumbach pictures them in bright yellow. It seems probable that other colors were used, too. *Thornburg Collection.*

These are the *Wee Piggys, Wee Piggy Girl* and *Wee Piggy Boy,*
according to the 1952 catalog, which also states they were made
in one color scheme only. The girl stands 3 3/8 inches high, the
boy 3 1/4 inches. Both are marked. Both are made of flesh color
bisque. *Schneider Collection.*

The *Wee Piggys* separated.

This guy is called *Goat,* according to the 1952 catalog. The marked piece is 4 1/8 inches high. Originally he had a paper sweet pea blossom in his mouth. *King Collection.*

Meet *Daisy Donkey,* 4 7/8 inches high with a Ceramic Arts Studio mark. In the 1954 catalog she was pictured next to *Elsie Elephant,* who is shown immediately below. *King Collection.*

Elsie Elephant, measuring 4 3/4 x 4 3/4, and unmarked. *Schneider Collection.*

Both of these donkeys are marked, but I forgot to record their heights. If memory serves me correct, they are about 2 1/2 and 3 inches high. *Thornburg Collection.*

That's Rep on the left, Dem on the right. Rep is 4 inches high, Dem wasn't measured. Both have Ceramic Arts Studio marks. *Thornburg Collection.*

That's it for domestic and farm animals, now onto wild animals if indeed a mouse can be considered wild. Called *Mouse and Cheese* in the 1952 catalog, this must have been one of the company's best sellers if the number available on today's secondary market is any indication. They seem to be all over the place. The *Mouse* is 2 inches high, the *Cheese* is 1 1/2 x 2 3/4. Each is marked. *Schneider Collection.*

These are the three animals that go with the Indian Group that is shown together on page 33. The *Bunny* is 1 7/8 inches high, the *Fawn,* 3 1/4 inches, and the *Chipmunk,* 2 inches. All three are marked; all are made of tan bisque. The *Bunny* was also made in white with pink highlights. *King Collection.*

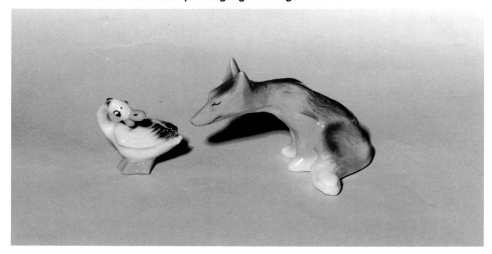

The fox and goose, 3 1/4 inches high and 2 inches high, respectively. Both are marked. *Weaver Collection.*

This set is generally called the kissing bunnies. They are unmarked, 4 and 2 1/8 inches high. *Thornburg Collection.*

These running rabbits are 4 inches high, unmarked. But they are not a true pair. The mate is somewhat shorter, about 3 inches high. *Thornburg Collection.*

The stylized doe in brown, 3 7/8 inches high with a Ceramic Arts Studio mark. Both this figure and its mate, the stylized fawn, are shown in olive in Chapter 2 Identification. *Schneider Collection.*

The bears are 1 3/4 and 3 1/2 inches high, marked, and made of tan slip the same color as the highlights. *Schneider Collection.*

The *Mother* and *Baby Skunk,* 3 5/8 inches and 1 7/8 inches, respectively. Both are marked. *Schneider Collection.*

Here is a skunk family plus one. The plus one is the *Skunky Bank* at far right, 4 inches high. The 1954 catalog suggested using it not only as a bank, but also as a flower holder. Now to the family. *Mrs. Skunk* is at top left, *Mr. Skunk* at top center. Each is 2 7/8 inches high. *Baby Boy Skunk,* 2 3/8 inches high, is the little guy in front with his tail up. He was also called *Inky* in the catalog. *Baby Girl Skunk (Dinky)* next to him stands 2 inches high. If you ever see her be sure to turn her over and look at the detailed pads on her front paws. None of the pieces in this picture are marked. *King Collection.*

This is called the *Squirrel* in the 1952 catalog. It is 2 1/4 inches high, and marked. According to the catalog, it was made in only one color scheme. It always looks to me like he is holding a microphone and singing, but that is not the case. *Oravitz Collection.*

The *Young Camel* salt and pepper shakers are each 5 5/8 inches high. Both are marked, a Ceramic Arts Studio mark on one front foot, a copyright symbol on the other. Although they look different because they were set at different angles for the photograph, you will want to note that a pair of *Young Camels* consists of two pieces made from identical molds. *Thornburg Collection.*

The *Young Camel* in green. According to the 1952 catalog, this was also made in grey. Size and marks are the same as above. *Schneider Collection.*

When it comes to quality, I think I would put these fighting leopards up against Beswick, Goebel, Royal Doulton or practically any other foreign pottery that status conscious name droppers seem to think did better work that our American firms. In my opinion, to say they are exquisite would be an understatement. The leopard on the left measures 2 3/4 x 6, the one on the right 3 1/4 x 4. Both are marked. As you can see, the head of the one on the left fits snugly into the paws of the one on the right. I don't suggest displaying them that way, however, as it would be too easy for someone unfamiliar to think they were one piece and accidentally break them while attempting to pick them up. This, incidentally, is a small set. They were also made in a larger size about half again as big. *Schneider Collection.*

The stylized lions measure 3 1/4 x 7 1/4 inches and 1 3/4 x 5 1/4. Both are marked. *Thornburg Collection.*

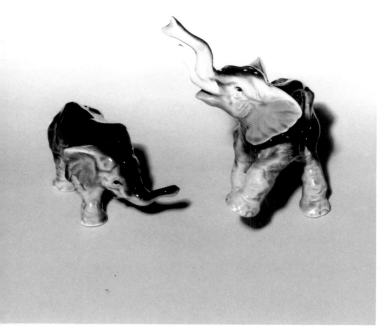

This is *Tembo* and *Tembino*. *Tembo* is the taller, 6 3/4 inches high. *Tembino* is the shorter, 2 1/2 inches high. Both are marked. *Thornburg Collection.*

Benny, or *Baby Elephant,* in yellow. Height is 3 5/8 inches. The piece is unmarked. *Schneider Collection.*

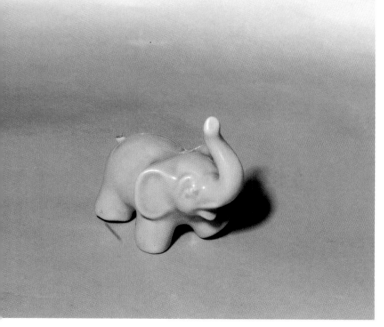

This elephant is called both *Annie* and *Large Elephant* in the 1954 catalog. Her companion is *Benny,* shown below. *Annie,* described as the mother, is 3 5/8 inches high and marked. *King Collection.*

Unmarked Ceramic Arts Studio *Giraffes* called *Young Giraffe* and *Large Giraffe* in the 1952 catalog. The *Large Giraffe,* on the left, stands 6 1/4 inches while the *Young Giraffe* measures in at 5 3/4. According to the catalog, they were also made with a combination of copper green and black glazes. *Thornburg Collection.*

The 1954 catalog shows that the *Monkey Family* was composed of three members--*Mr. Monk, Mrs. Monk* and *Baby Monk*. This picture shows *Mrs. Monk* and *Baby Monk,* 3 1/2 and 1 7/8 inches high, respectively. Neither is marked. These were made in white and black, and black and white as shown below. *Schneider Collection.*

The white and black monkey on the right looks like a repeat of above but that's not the case. Both of these are *Mr. Monk,* 4 1/8 inches high, and unmarked. *Oravitz Collection.*

The panda is 2 3/4 inches high, has a Ceramic Arts Studio mark. Looks to me like he would be a good partner for the *Squirrel* on page 80 that appears to be singing. *King Collection.*

These marked *Zebras* are 5 1/2 inches high. Like the *Young Camels* above, a pair is made up of two pieces exactly alike. Laumbach pictures them in black and amber, the only other color combination made, according to the 1952 catalog. *Thornburg Collection.*

Of all the nesting animals, the *Bears* are the most common. The *Mother* is 4 1/2 inches high, the *Baby* 2 1/4 inches. The brown pair looks like a married set, each of them coming from a different run at the factory. Not so. Just about all of the brown *Bears* I have seen, and that's a considerable number, have a dark *Mother* and light *Baby.* Maybe it was done so people would realize they were two separate pieces when they picked them up. I have talked to three very reliable people who say they have these *Bears* in black but I have never personally seen them. *Schneider Collection.*

If you are already a collector of Ceramic Arts Studio figures you have probably noticed that some sets seem to have a way of eluding you no matter how close you get to them. That is what has happened to Cindy and me with the *Mother* and *Baby Bunnies*. Our friend, Susan Oravitz, purchased the pair in this picture just three booths up from ours at a flea market for $3. Not long after that another friend bought a pair for $4 at a different flea market at which we were set up. The *Mother* is 4 1/2 inches high, the *Baby* 2 1/4 inches. Both are marked. *Oravitz Collection.*

According to the 1952 catalog, these are the only two colors for the *Mother* and *Baby Kangaroos*. The *Mother* stands 4 3/4 inches, the *Baby* 2 3/8 inches. The catalog suggests using the yellow *Baby* with the grey *Mother* or the grey *Baby* with the yellow *Mother,* something I have never tried but which I think might look rather nice. Taking into consideration that the catalog suggested mixing the colors, if you happen to find a set made up of both colors it seems likely they may have been sold that way originally. *King Collection.*

I often see this set of *Cows* with the *Mother's* horns broken. The *Mother* is 5 1/4 inches high, the *Calf* 2 1/4 inches high. Both are marked. *King Collection.*

The mother gorilla is 4 inches high, the Baby 2 1/2 inches. Each is marked. *Schneider Collection.*

The simplest of the Ceramic Arts Studio birds is this one-piece set of *Lovebirds.* Unmarked, they measure 2 1/2 inches high, 5 inches wide. *Oravitz Collection.*

Chapter 14: Birds

You can roughly divide Ceramic Arts Studio birds into two categories, shelf sitters and non-shelf sitters. Most of the non-shelf sitters are fairly easy to find. The shelf sitters are not only harder to find, but often when you do run into them you discover they have been repaired, sometimes quite extensively.

I have a theory about why that is. My belief is that many of these shelf sitting birds sat on window sills or sashes, the most natural place for them to be displayed. Most windows in the homes of that era were made of wood and opened up and down instead of side to side. They were opened and closed often during the summer in those days before air conditioning, sometimes requiring great effort to get them moving during periods of high humidity. Many homeowners used shades to block the sun, or the wide Venetian blinds that were popular then. All those potential perils considered, it is easy to see why perfect examples of Ceramic Arts Studio shelf sitting birds are in rather short supply today.

Most collectors I know find themselves purchasing repaired pieces with hopes of replacing them with perfect pieces at a later time.

Lovebirds in white, green and yellow. Laumbach shows them with dark blue highlights, and I assume they were probably made in several other color combinations. *Schneider Collection.*

The *Penguins, Mr. and Mrs.,* appeared in the 1952 catalog where they sold wholesale for $12 per dozen pairs. Although their looks are deceiving, each is the same height. That's 4 inches if we go by the measurements I took for *The Complete Salt and Pepper Shaker Book,* 3 3/4 inches if we use the measurements I took for this book. (Makes me feel a bit schizophrenic; can't figure out whether to believe me or me.) In any event, both *Penguins* are marked. *Thornburg Collection.*

The *Fighting Cocks* were not given specific names in the 1952 catalog other than that the one on the left was designated as the pepper and the one on the right the salt. Heights are 3 1/4 inches on the left, 3 7/8 inches on the right. Both are marked. *King Collection.*

Chirp, on the left, stands 3 3/4 inches high. *Twirp,* on the right, is slightly taller at 3 7/8 inches. Both are marked and named. Laumbach pictures a blue and yellow pair. *Thornburg Collection.*

A repeat of the above *Fighting Cocks* with a much darker reddish one. The same glaze was used on both pair, just applied thicker on this one. Some collectors consider these bona fide different examples worthy of inclusion in their collections, others do not. *Thornburg Collection.*

The shelf-sitting canaries measure 4 1/2 and 5 1/8 inches high. Both are marked. *King Collection.*

Pudgie is on the left, *Budgie* is on the right. *Budgie* is 6 inches high, *Pudgie* was not measured but is about the same. Each is marked and named. *King Collection.*

Canaries from the front.

Pudgie and *Budgie* from the front.

Pete is on the left, 8 1/8 inches high. Polly is on the right, 7 7/8 inches. Both are marked and named. *King Collection.*

Budgie in aqua and grey, same size and marks as above. *Schneider Collection.*

Pete and Polly in green and yellow. *Schneider Collection.*

The fish on the left is 3 1/2 inches high, the one on the right 3 3/4 inches. Both are marked. The 1952 catalog called them *Fish Head Up* and *Fish Head Down,* and said they came in two color schemes, green or golden amber. *King Collection.*

Chapter 15: Aquatic Creatures

This is a short chapter because Ceramic Arts Studio didn't offer a lot of variety in this category. What it did make is generally quite nice and worth including in any collection.

The 1954 catalog referred to these fish by two different sets of names--*Swish and Swirl,* and *Twist Tail* and *Straight Tail. Swish (Twist Tail)* is 2 inches high, *Swirl (Straight Tail),* is 3 inches high. Neither is marked. *King Collection.*

The *Toadstool* stands 2 3/8 inches high, the *Frog* 2 inches. Both are marked, and the *Toadstool* is made of yellow bisque. The *Toadstool* appears again in Chapter 16 with an *Elf* sitting under it. *Thornburg Collection.*

While many objects look better in a photograph than they do in real life, that's not the case with this set. The camera seems to take something away from it. The *Seahorse* is 3 1/2 inches high, the *Coral* 3 1/8 inches. Both are marked. Their description in the 1952 catalog implies that that was the first year they were offered. *King Collection.*

Seahorse and *Coral* in yellow and sea green. *Weaver Collection.*

SECTION IV: Fantasies

Ceramic Arts Studio's venture into fantasyland was rather limited in scope, the company producing less than a dozen different designs of pixies, elves and sprites. But these pieces represent some of the studio's best work in the field of putting ornate, intricate decoration on small figures. Settle back in your easy chair for a short yet satisfying cruise through fantasyland Ceramic Arts Studio style, and you'll probably find the trip well worth your time.

Chapter 16: Pixies and Elves

All of these pieces were very nicely executed with the exception of the oak sprites, Oakie and Dokie, which often look and feel rather rough. The detailed hand painting that is prevalent on most of the pixies was reflected in their prices. *Toadstool Pixie*, for instance, sold in 1952 for $12 per dozen wholesale, the same price charged for the much larger *Mo-Pi* and *Smi-Li* Chinese figures shown in Chapter 9.

The two-piece *Elf* and *Toadstool* set is made of yellow bisque. The *Toadstool* measures 2 1/4 inches in height, the *Elf*, 2 inches. Both are marked. *Thornburg Collection.*

Called *Toadstool Pixie,* this chap stands 4 inches high. The piece is not marked. *Oravitz Collection.*

Peak-a-boo Pixie, 2 3/4 inches high and unmarked. *Oravitz Collection.*

Toadstool Pixie in a different color scheme. Also a slightly different size, 3 7/8 inches. Small variations in the sizes of like pieces generally occur for one of two reasons, neither of which is usually intentional. The first is that sometimes the original block used to make the mold must be recarved because it was accidentally damaged, destroyed, lost or misplaced, and the finished product comes out a little smaller or larger. The second is called mold growth, the natural erosion that occurs when a mold is used longer than it should be. Usually this results only in loss of detail, but in extreme cases pieces made from old molds will come out slightly larger. Vanity is a third possibility--I may have been wearing my glasses to read the tape measure at one photo session, not wearing them at another. *Schneider Collection.*

Riding Pixie, another unmarked entry, stands 2 3/4 inches high. In the 1954 catalog, *Riding Pixie, Peak-a-boo Pixie* and *Toadstool Pixie* were grouped together and advertised as *Piquant Pixies. Schneider Collection.*

Riding Pixie in a different color scheme. *Oravitz Collection.*

Waving Pixie is 2 1/8 inches high, unmarked. In the 1954 catalog, this piece was described as a little girl pixie, and was coupled with *Kneeling Pixie,* another little girl pixie who was carrying a mushroom on her shoulder. Note that *Waving Pixie* shows up in the two pictures immediately below. *Schneider Collection.*

This *Pixie Tray* measures 3 1/4 inches high, 5 1/2 inches side to side, 5 3/4 inches front to back. It is not marked. The 1954 catalog showed not only this one fused to a bowl, but also her partner *Kneeling Pixie* and all three *Piquant Pixies*. Blue, green, and rose were stated as the color combinations. *Oravitz Collection.*

Pixie Tray in rose and yellow. Note that *Waving Pixie* herself is also a different color than the one above. *King Collection.*

I didn't find these in the catalogs, but Wellman refers to them as Oakie on a spring leaf and Dokie on a fall leaf. Oakie is 2 1/4 inches high, Dokie 2 5/8 inches high. The leaf is 3 3/4 inches long. All of the pieces are marked. *Thornburg Collection.*

SECTION V: Posy Pots

During the 1950s, and into the 1960s, many domestic potteries and importers did a booming business selling figural vases to both the florist trade and department stores. Judging by the large number you see at antique shows today, head vases were especially lucrative. Those who ran Ceramic Arts Studio obviously recognized the trend and cashed in on it to at least a limited extent.

That's *Bonnie* on the left, *Barbie* on the right. Each is 7 1/4 inches high, each is marked and named. *Schneider Collection.*

Chapter 17: Planters and Vases

While the prices of the bud vases shown in this chapter are still quite reasonable, the prices of the head vases have risen sharply in recent years as more and more people have begun collecting these curiosities. As with any other collectible, increased demand spawned by cross-competition results in less availability and higher prices. If there is any subtle satisfaction to be had by this situation, it is that head vase collectors' willingness to pay higher prices for Ceramic Arts Studio examples than for imported pieces shows they obviously appreciate the higher quality of American ceramics.

So why show a picture the same as that directly above? Because it's not the same, that's why. Look closely and you will see hand decoration on *Bonnie's* left shoulder, an adornment that carries over to the top of her hat, which appears on the next page. As stated earlier, some collectors consider these types of little differences make two completely different pieces and search for examples of each. Others feel the difference is not that great and are satisfied to have only one. *King Collection.*

Hand decoration on *Bonnie's* hat.

Mei-Ling looks more like a figure but is actually a vase having two holes in the head that do not show in the picture. *Mei-Ling* stands 5 inches high, is marked and named. *Schneider Collection.*

Barbie in rose and white with black hair. *Schneider Collection.*

Lotus, on the left, is 7 7/8 inches high. *Manchu,* on the right, is 7 1/2 inches. Both are marked and named. *Schneider Collection.*

According to the 1952 catalog, *Becky*, 5 1/8 inches high, came not only with the brown hair shown here and the blonde hair shown on the Contents page, but also with black hair. Like other Ceramic Arts Studio head vases, *Becky* is marked and named. *King Collection.*

On the left is *Sven*, 6 3/8 inches high. His companion is *Svea*, 5 3/4 inches. Both pieces are marked and named. *Schneider Collection.*

Sven with brown hair and light green trim. These vases were also made with blonde hair. *King Collection.*

The Wing-Sang and Lu-Tang bamboo bud vases are probably the most common of all of the Ceramic Arts Studio vases. The Wing-Sang vase on the left stands 7 inches high while the Lu-Tang vase, on the right, stands 6 5/8 inches. Both have Betty Harrington/Ceramic Arts Studio marks. Wing-Sang and Lu-Tang were also made as freestanding figurines as shown in Chapter 2. The bamboo bud vases were made separately, too. *Schneider Collection.*

While I have seen many Wing-Sang and Lu-Tang bamboo bud vases, I believe this is the only pair I have ever seen in white. Sizes and marks are the same as above. *King Collection.*

This Loreli planter measures 6 1/2 x 6 inches. It has a Betty Harrington/Ceramic Arts Studio inkstamp. *Schneider Collection.*

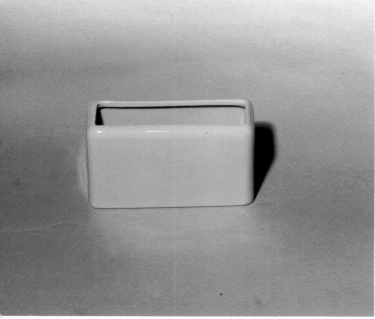

Who'd a thunk it, a very plain piece of Ceramic Arts Studio pottery. I'm sure if I had seen this 2 1/2 x 4 3/8 inch planter in a mall or at a show I would not even have picked it up. That would have been my tough luck, however, because on the bottom there is a Ceramic Arts Studio mark along with "#454 Planter Pot," as shown at right. *King Collection.*

Bottom of above yellow planter.

Cindy and I thought these were rather dull looking when we saw them on Wellman's video. But when we viewed them in person we were awestruck by their clean lines, simple beauty and imposing size. As you can see, they were made to be vases or wallpockets. The one on the left, 8 1/2 inches high, has "African Lady / Plaque / Ceramic Arts Studio / Madison, Wisc. / ©" incised on five lines. The one on the right, 8 1/4 inches high, has the same mark except that it says "Man" instead of "Lady." *King Collection.*

SECTION VI: Decorating the Walls

It seems somewhat of a paradox that most homes have much more wall space than counter or shelf space, yet most potteries made many times more sitting objects than hanging ones. While you will find only a limited number of Ceramic Arts Studio wall plaques in Chapter 18, each and every one of them will be of the high quality you have come to expect after reading this far.

Chapter 18: Wall Plaques

If someone wanted to specialize in collecting a specific type of Ceramic Arts Studio's output, wall plaques would have a lot going for them. The two big reasons are that display space is plentiful in most homes, and chances of breakage are less than with figurines. After all, a wall is a pretty safe place compared to a shelf, window sill, counter top or even a crowded china cabinet.

Another nice thing about collecting wall plaques is that you are getting Ceramic Arts Studio's top shelf items. Leaf through the 1952 catalog and you will find that wall plaques are the most expensive things in it, *Grace* and *Greg*, and *Attitude* and *Arabesque*, each bringing $30 per dozen pieces. In the same catalog the *Elephant* and *Boy* sold for $12 per dozen pairs. Today, from a knowledgeable dealer, that once low-priced *Elephant* and *Boy* will run you $150 to $200 while the originally higher priced *Attitude* and *Arabesque* would require a cash outlay of about only $40 to $60.

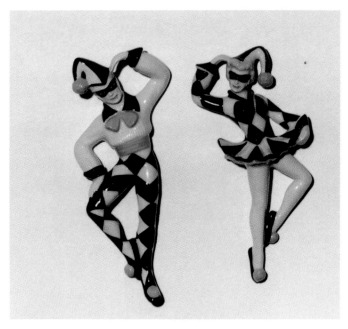

The plaque on the left measures 8 7/8 inches, the one on the right 8 1/2 inches. Both have Ceramic Arts Studio marks along with the name *Harlequin* on the man and *Columbine* on the woman. *Schneider Collection.*

Harlequin and Columbine in red. Yellow was also made, possibly other colors, too. Schneider Collection.

Grace and Greg in blue. When you see these figures you must look closely because the colors tend to look the same when not making a side-by-side comparison. King Collection.

Grace and Greg are 8 3/4 and 9 1/4 inches, respectively. They are made of flesh color bisque, and each is marked and named. Schneider Collection.

Greg in chartreuse. The blue is a repeat of above. Schneider Collection.

Attitude and Arabesque. Attitude (left) is 9 inches high, Arabesque (right) 9 1/2 inches. Like the green and gold pair shown on page 5, each is marked and named and made of flesh color bisque. *Schneider Collection.*

Same plaques in white and red, and also separated. *King Collection.*

The *Dutch Boy Plaque* measures 8 1/4 inches in length, the *Dutch Girl Plaque* 7 3/4 inches. Both are marked and named. When you see this *Dutch Boy Plaque* in person you realize how vivid Ceramic Arts Studio's blue glaze was. *Schneider Collection.*

This is the *Chinese Lantern Man,* his name appearing on the back along with a Ceramic Arts Studio mark. He is 8 inches high. His lantern is a separate piece that is often missing. *Schneider Collection.*

The *Chinese Lantern Woman* minus the lantern and gold trim of the man. The plaque is marked the same but was not measured. *King Collection.*

On the left is Neptune, 5 3/4 x 4 3/8 inches. Water Sprite is on the right, 4 3/8 x 5 3/8 inches. Both are marked. According to Wellman, Mermaid, the same size as Neptune, is Neptune's true partner. The Water Sprite shown here is Water Sprite Fish Up (in her hands), her partner being Water Sprite Fish Down. *King Collection.*

Zor and *Zorina*, both 9 inches long and marked and named. These are shown in ivory on page 14. *King Collection.*

Each of these plaques is 7 1/2 inches long. They are marked *Shadow Dancer A* and *Shadow Dancer B,* along with their Ceramic Arts Studio marks. Laumbach shows one of them in a blackish-grey color. *King Collection.*

That's *Cockatoo Plaque B* on the left, 8 1/4 inches from comb to tail. *Cockatoo Plaque A* is on the right. Comb to tail measurement on *A* is 7 7/8 inches. Both are marked and named. *Schneider Collection.*

SECTION VII: *Miscellaneous*

This section covers all of the things that aren't in the other sections. They include banks, pitchers, ashtrays, candleholders and a few others. You might view them as the pieces that round out a Ceramic Arts Studio collection.

Chapter 19: Candleholders, Pitchers, Banks, Etc.

A lot of collectors tell me they seldom find some of the things shown in this chapter such as miniature jasperware pitchers and toby jugs. I don't think that is so much because the items are unavailable as that people just don't see them. Let's face it. When you go out looking for Ceramic Arts Studio your mind is generally keyed to figurines, head vases and wall plaques. Pitchers and the like are for other collectors. In my own searching I have found three pitchers, but each one of them was on my third or fourth pass, by which time I was going slower and studying things more carefully.

Some collectors, my wife included, choose not to collect the non-figural items. Those who do wish to acquire them should be able to do so if they just remember to look for them.

Each of these candle holders is 5 inches high. In addition to their Ceramic Arts Studio marks, the bottoms also contain their names which are, not surprisingly, *See No Evil, Hear No Evil* and *Speak No Evil. Oravitz Collection.*

Candle holders in light blue, sizes and marks the same. *King Collection.*

A small toby pitcher, 3 1/4 inches high, and marked. *King Collection.*

This set is called the triad candle holders. Note that it is in two different color schemes. Heights left to right are 6 3/4, 5 3/8 and 6 3/4 inches. Each piece is marked. *King Collection.*

Laumbach calls this the boy and girl with apple pitcher, Wellman calls it the Adam and Eve pitcher with twig handle. It is 3 inches high, has a Ceramic Arts Studio mark, and is made of green bisque. *King Collection.*

This pine motif disk pitcher stands 3 1/2 inches high and bears a Ceramic Arts Studio mark. *King Collection.*

Two more jasperware-like pitchers. The George Washington pitcher on the left stands 3 inches high, while the Diana pitcher on the right is slightly taller at 3 1/8 inches. Mark information was not recorded. *King Collection.*

Made in the image of jasperware, the swan pitcher stands 3 inches high while the horse pitcher stands 2 inches. Both are marked. *King Collection.*

This razor bank is 4 7/8 inches high, carries a Ceramic Arts Studio mark on its bottom along with the words *Barber Head.* The 1952 catalog referred to it by that name, and also *Tony the Barber. Schneider Collection.*

These swear banks were called *Blankety Blank Man* and *Blankety Blank Woman* in the 1952 catalog, which also said they were finished in green only. He is 4 1/2 inches high, she is 4 1/4 inches high. Each is marked. *King Collection.*

The hippopotamus ashtray measures 3 1/4 x 4 1/4 inches. Mark information was not recorded. *King Collection.*

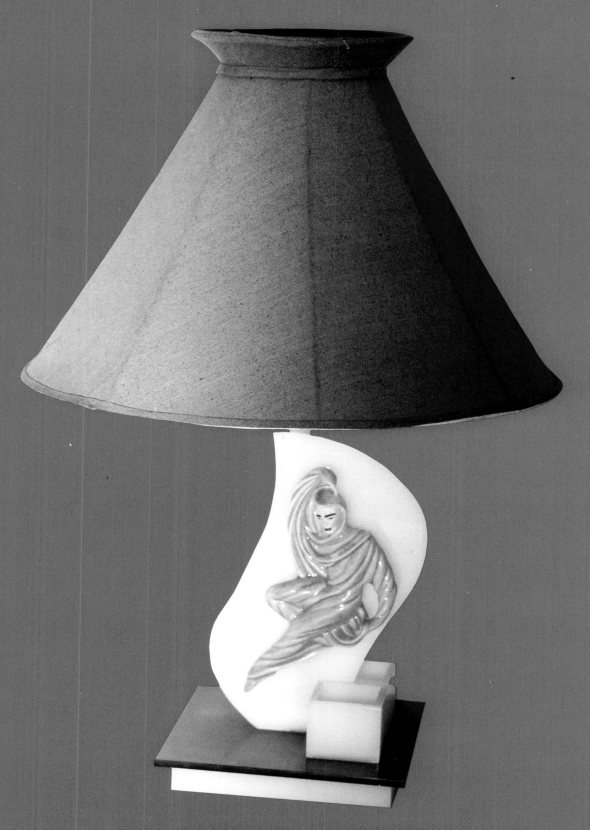

According to Wellman, lamp companies used Ceramic Arts Studio pieces to decorate their wares. My own feeling is that this example with *Zor* on it was probably one of a pair, the other having the plastic curving the opposite direction with *Zorina* attached to it. *Schneider Collection.*

Appendix: Sources

Harrington Figurines, Sabra Olson Laumbach. $19.95 plus $2 postage Order from: Sabra Olson Laumbach c/o Antiques Minnesota, Inc., 1516 E. Lake St., Minneapolis, MN 55407

Ceramic Arts Studio Collectors Club
c/o Jim Petzold
Po. Box 46
Madison Wi, 53701
Enclose $15 Dues

All of the materials listed below may be ordered from: Rags to Riches Antiques & Collectibles, BA Wellman, #9 Cottage St., Southboro, MA 01772-1907. Postage is included in the following prices.

Current *Ceramic Arts Studio Price Guide*, $7.95.
Ceramic Arts Studio Video Book I
   (VHS format), $18.95.
Ceramic Arts Studio Video Book II
   (VHS format), $18.95.
1952 Ceramic Arts Studio Catalog, reprint,
   (8 1/2" x 5 1/2"), $12.
1954 Ceramic Arts Studio Catalog, reprint
   (8 1/2" x 11"), $12.

Bibliography

Laumbach, Sabra Olson, *Harrington Figurines*, Ferguson Communications, Hillsdale, Michigan, 1985.

Schneider, Mike, *Animal Figures*, Schiffer Publishing Ltd., West Chester, Pennsylvania, 1990.

-----, *Complete Salt and Pepper Shaker Book, The*, Schiffer Publishing Ltd., Atglen, Pennsylvania, 1993.

-----, "Harrington Molded Vision of World Culture," *Antique Week*, July 22, 1991.

Wellman, BA, *Ceramic Arts Studio 1952 Catalog* reprint.

-----, *Ceramic Arts Studio 1954 Catalog* reprint.

-----, *Ceramic Arts Studio 1992-93 Price Guide*, self-published, Southboro, Massachusetts, 1992.

-----, *Ceramic Arts Studio Video Book I*, self-published, Southboro, Massachusetts.

-----, *Ceramic Arts Studio Video Book II*, self-published, Southboro, Massachusetts.

Price Guide

The dollar amounts shown below should not be construed as hard and fast prices, but rather as general guidelines to help you interpret relative value when comparing one piece to another. For example, the first two values shown, $185 for *Alice* and the *March Hare*, and $25 for the *Fish*, may vary some from locality to locality, but the former will always be significantly more valuable than the latter. The largest local variation will probably be within about a 50 mile radius of Madison, Wisconsin, where prices often run quite a bit higher than in most of the rest of the country.

Prices correspond to pieces in excellent condition even if those appearing in the book are not. Prices are for the number of pieces shown unless otherwise stated. In other words, in the example above the $185 listed for *Alice* and the *March Hare* is for the pair, not for each piece. Also, the prices are based on the value of figurines regardless of whether figurines or shakers are shown in the pictures. For shakers add 20 percent.

Further information about prices appears in Chapter 4 Values.

Harem Girl Sitting $45
49 *Comedy* and *Tragedy* $120
   Comedy $60
50 *Bruce* and *Beth* $60
   Maurice and *Michelle* $50
   Dance Moderne Man and *Woman* $100
51 *Pensive* and *Blythe* $160
   Flutist and *Lutist* $200
   Water Man and *Woman* $160
52 *Fire Man* $80
   Fire Man and *Woman* $160
   Grace and *Greg* (sitters) $90
53 *Ballet En Pose* and *En Repose* $75
   Rose $45
   Daisy $45
54 *Pierette* and *Pierrot* $110
   Bass Viol Boy $45
55 *Guitar Boy* $45
   Accordian Boy $45
   Banjo Girl $45
   Harmonica Boy $45
   Flute Girl $45
56 *Harmonica Boy* $45
   Sax Boy $45
   Drum Girl $45
57 Madonna $40
   Angel Praying $30
   Angel Sleeping $30
58 *Angel Arm Down* $40
   Angel with candle $30
   Angel Arm Up $40
   Angel standing with star $35
   Angel singing $35
59 *Cinderella* and *Prince*
   Blonde hair $130
   Black Hair $100
60 *Wendy* and *Peter Pan* $140   *Hansel and Gretel* (one-piece) $35
   Sambo and tiger
     Sambo $300
     Tiger $50
61 *Running Girl* $30
   Running Boy $30
   Praying Girl $30
   Jack Horner
     no. 1 $45
     no. 2 $45
     no. 3 $45
   Miss Muffet
     no. 1 $45
     no. 2 $45
     no. 3 $45
62 *Little Boy Blue* $15
   Little Bo Peep $20
   Mary and *Lamb* $40
   Mary $25
63 *Paul Bunyan* and tree
   Paul Bunyan $65
   Tree $15
   Santa Claus and tree $50
   St. George on Charger $150
   Lady Rowena on Charger $150
64 *Archibald the Dragon* $120
   Cupid $60
65 *Fufu* $25
   Sooty and *Taffy* $40
   Pom Sitting and *Pom Standing* $45
66 *Billy* and *Butch* $45
   Spaniels $40
67 One-piece Scotties $35

Collie shelf sitter $35
Collie pups $20 each
68 *Sitting* and *Standing Cocker* $45
   Standing Cocker $25
   Dog and doghouse $40
69 Unnamed puppy $25
   Thai and *Thai-Thai* $45
   Gingham Dog and *Calico Cat* $35
70 Large Cat $35
   Tomcat $35
   Kitten Washing $15
   Sleeping Kitten $15
   Washing Kitten $15
   Scratching Kitten $15
71 Stylized black cats $80
   Stylized brown cat $45
   Tom Cat $35
   Bright Eyes $30
72 *Thunder* and *Lightning* $125
   Palomino Colt $45
   Balky Colt $30
73 Horseheads $30 per pair
74 Ox and covered wagon $75
   Modern lambs $35
75 *Wee Piggy Boy* and *Girl* $30
76 *Goat* $40
   Daisy Donkey $35
   Elsie Elephant $35
77 Unnamed donkeys $75
   Dem and Rep $55
   Mouse and *Cheese* $15
78 *Bunny* $25
   Fawn $40
   Chipmunk $25
   Fox and goose $65
   Kissing bunnies $50
79 Running Rabbits $45 per true pair
   Stylized doe $40
   Bears $65
80 *Mother* and *Baby Skunk* $45
   Skunky Bank $75
   Mrs. Skunk $35
   Mr. Skunk $35
   Inky $20
   Dinky $20
   Squirrel $30
81 *Young Camels* $110
   Young Camel $55
82 Fighting leopards $140
   Stylized lions $120
83 *Tembo* and *Tembino* $100
   Annie and *Benny* $35
   Giraffes $140
84 *Mrs. Monk* $35
   Baby Monk $25
   Mr. Monk $35
   Panda $35
85 Zebras $140
   Mother and baby bear
     White $45
     Brown $35
86 *Mother* and *Baby Bunny* $60
   Cows $85
   Mother and *Baby Kangaroo* $45
   Mother and baby gorilla $60
87 *Lovebirds* $20
88 *Mr.* and *Mrs. Penguin* $40
   Chirp and *Twirp* $50
   Fighting Cocks $45
89 Canaries $50

Pudgie and *Budgie* $50
90 *Budgie* $25
   Pete and *Polly* $70
91 *Fish Head Up* and
     Fish Head Down $40
   Swish and *Swirl* $25
   Toadstool and *Frog* $40
92 *Seahorse* and *Coral* $60
93 *Elf* and *Toadstool* $45
94 *Toadstool Pixie* $35
   Peek-A-Boo Pixie $35
95 *Riding Pixie* $35
   Waving Pixie $35
96 *Pixie Tray* $35
   Oakie on spring leaf $25
   Dokie on fall leaf $25
97 *Bonnie* and *Barbie* $90
   Bonnie $45
98 *Barbie* $45
   Mei-Ling $55 each
   Lotus and *Manchu* $100
99 *Becky* $75
   Sven and *Svea* $140
   Sven $70
100 Wing-Sang and Lu-Tang
     bud vases $35 each
   Loreli planter $75
101 #454 Planter Pot $15
   African Man and *Lady Plaques* $300
102 *Harlequin* and *Columbine* $110
103 *Harlequin* and *Columbine* $110
   Grace and *Greg* $80
104 *Attitude* and *Arabesque* $65
   Dutch Boy and *Girl Plaques* $90
   Chinese Lantern Man Plaque
     (with lantern) $40
105 *Chinese Lantern Woman*
     Plaque (without lantern) $35
   Zor and *Zorina* $50
   Shadow Dancers A and *B* $70
   Neptune $75
   Water Sprite Fish Up $45
   Cockatoo Plaques A and *B* $60
106 See, hear and speak no evil
     candleholders $35 each
107 See, hear and speak no evil
     candleholders $35 each
   Triad console set $50 each piece
   Small Toby pitcher $40
   Adam and Eve pitcher $35
108 Disk pitcher $25
   Swan pitcher $25
   Horsehead creamer $25
   Barber Head razor bank $65
   George Washington pitcher $25
   Diana pitcher $25
   Blankety Blank Man and *Woman*
     swear banks $130
   Hippopotamus ashtray $35
109 Zor lamp $150

Other Books From Schiffer Publishing